Association for Jewish Youth
Norwood House
Harmony Way
Off Victoria Road
London NW4 4BZ
Tel: 0181 203 3030
Fax: 0181 202 3030

112670

Challenge

CHALLENGE

an encounter with Lubavitch—Chabad in Israel

PUBLISHED BY THE LUBAVITCH FOUNDATION OF GREAT BRITAIN

Original artwork by Baruch Nachshon.

Photography by Micha Bar Am
and Isaac Freidin

Printed in Great Britain by Jarrold & Sons Ltd, Norwich

Rabbi Menachem M. Schneerson

THE LUBAVITCHER REBBE שליט"א

RABBI MENACHEM M. SCHNEERSON
Lubavitch
770 Eastern Parkway
Brooklyn 13, N. Y.

HYacinth 3-9250

מנחם מענדל שניאורסאהן
ליובאוויטש

770 איסטערן פאַרקוויי
ברוקלין, נ. י.

By the Grace of G-d
11th of Nissan, 5732
Brooklyn, N.Y.

To the Sons and Daughters of
Our People Israel, Everywhere

      G-d bless you all

Greeting and Blessing:

In these days on the eve of Pesach, the festival that marks the "birth" and
initiation of our Jewish people, one's mind turns to reflect on the question:
What and how should be this nation's way of life in order that it realize, in
the surest and best possible manner, the purpose and goal of its
existence?

This is a broad and multi-faceted subject, and only one aspect of it will
be dwelt upon here: Should this nation strive toward a state of life in
which it can enjoy the maximum pleasure with the minimum effort; or -
should it prefer a life of toil and maximum achievement, a life of much
action and much accomplishment?

The question is just as pertinent to the individual and his personal life
as an individual.

Needless to say, this is not an abstract question, for in resolving this
question one way or the other, the foundation is laid for the individual's
concept of the pattern of his life, and how he will respond to what is
happening to him and around him, even in matters not directly relating to
him, and certainly in matters which directly affect his life.

*   *   *

At first glance, and on the basis of our faith and our Torah, called
Toras Chaim and Toras Emes ("Law of Life" and "Law of Truth"), by
which we are committed to the principle that the Creator and Master of
the world, - including the "small world," namely, man - is the Essence of
Goodness, and that "it is the nature of the Good to do good," it would
appear reasonable to suppose that the highest perfection is to be found in a
state where the maximum pleasure - true pleasure - is obtainable without
difficulties and without travail; for in such a state "the nature of the Good
to do good" would be perceived in fullest measure.

Yet, the Torah, which is Torah - Or (showing things in their true essence), declares, "Man is unto travail born."

Even the first man (Adam), and before his downfall, was placed in the Garden of Eden with the assigned task "to till it and guard it," and only after that did G-d tell him "of all the trees of the Garden you may eat."

The explanation of the matter, which also resolves the apparent contradiction indicated above, is also given in the Torah:

Precisely because G-d desires that man should enjoy the good in its perfection, and human nature is such that a person derives true pleasure only if he is a partner in its attainment, through his own exertion and travail; whereas, on the contrary, if he receives it entirely gratis it is degrading to him, as though he was receiving charity ("bread of shame") - precisely because of this, the good in its perfection is enjoyed only when a person earns it through hard work, and the harder the effort, the sweeter tastes the fruit of achievement.

*   *   *

This is how it was at the birth of our Jewish nation. The plan of Yetzias Mitzraim (liberation from Egypt) was revealed in G-d's words to Moshe Rabbeinu: "When you will take out the people from Egypt, you (all) will serve G-d at this mountain (Sinai)." To be sure, Yetzias Mitzraim itself was an act of Heavenly grace, and in a manner of wonderful and obvious miracles. However, it was conditioned from the start on serving G-d (as a hard-working servant). This was the contribution of the nation, its participation in its newly won liberty from Egyptian bondage.

*   *   *

And as it is with the Jewish nation as a whole, so it is with the individual. A person's striving should be to act and to achieve results; and not merely to act, but to do so with exertion, in terms of "travail" as defined by Toras Emes. Only in this way does a man rise from the state of "Man (adam) being dust (adamah)" to the state of "Man (adam) emulating G-d (adameh l'Elyon).

*   *   *

Indeed, the birth and whole life of a person are constantly attended by miracles. Even when it appears that everything is proceeding in the "natural course", our Sages of blessed memory remind us that "a person is unaware of the miracle that happened to him." This is why we thank G-d three times a day, in our daily prayers, "For Your miracles that are with us every day."

So also David, the Sweetener of the Hymns of Israel (and King of Israel) declares on behalf of every Jew, and on behalf of all Israel: "From my mother's bowels You took me out (Midrash. This refers (also) to the delivery of the Jewish people from the power of Egypt).. I am a wonder to many (Midrash: Many miracles You have wrought for me)..I will enter into (the years of) strength..and to this day will I declare Your wondrous works (Midrash:..in every age, time, and moment)..You will revive me (Midrash: You will take me out of Exile)."

In conclusion: The entire life of a person, from birth and on, as also the entire history of our Jewish nation, thrives on continuous miracles (though these are not always clearly seen), which will culminate in the miracle of the true Geulo of the individual as well as of Klal Yisroel.

And by virtue of our actions and our service throughout the period of the Golus, in the daily life of both the individual and Klal, in compliance with the Divine imperative - the ultimate perfection of the whole world is being realized.

The true and complete Geulo through out righteous Moshiach, the fulfilment of the Prophetic promise:

"As in the days of your liberation from the land of Mitzraim, I will show you wonders."

With blessing for a
Kosher and happy Pesach

m. Schneerson

Contents

the founders of general Chassidism and the heads of Chabad

the Founder of Chassidism
Rabbi Israel Baal Shem Tov
Elul 18, 5458–*Sivan* 6, 5520 (1698–1760)

Successor
Rabbi Dovber of Meseritch
(Date of birth unknown)–*Kislev* 19, 5533 (?–1772)

Founder of Chabad
Rabbi Shneur Zalman of Ladi
Elul 18, 5505–*Teves* 24, 5573 (1745–1812)

Second Generation
Rabbi Dovber
(the son of Rabbi Shneur Zalman)
Kislev 9, 5534–*Kislev* 9, 5588 (1773–1827)

Third Generation
Rabbi Menachem Mendel
(grandson of Rabbi Shneur Zalman; son-in-law of Rabbi Dovber)
Elul 29, 5549–*Nissan* 13, 5626 (1789–1866)

Fourth Generation
Rabbi Shmuel
(son of Rabbi Menachem Mendel)
Iyar 2, 5594–*Tishrei* 13, 5643 (1834–1882)

Fifth Generation
Rabbi Sholom Dovber
(son of Rabbi Shmuel)
Cheshvan 20, 5621–*Nissan* 2, 5680 (1860–1920)

Sixth Generation
Rabbi Joseph Isaac Schneersohn
(son of Rabbi Sholom Dovber)
Tammuz 12, 5640–*Shevat* 10, 5710 (1880–1950)

Seventh Generation
Rabbi Menachem Mendel Schneerson שליט״א
(sixth in direct paternal line from Rabbi Menachem Mendel,
son-in-law of Rabbi Joseph Isaac)
Born *Nissan* 11, 5662 (1902)

"**B**ehold I have taught you statutes and judgements, even as the L–rd my G–d commanded me that you should do so in the midst of the land whither you go in to possess it.

Keep therefore and do them; for this is your wisdom and your understanding in the sight of the peoples, who shall hear all these statutes and say: 'Surely this great nation is a wise and understanding people.'

For what great nation is there, that has G–d so near unto them, as the L–rd our G–d is whenever we call upon Him?

And what great nation is there that has statutes and judgements so righteous as all this Law, which I set before you this day?"

Deuteronomy IV 5–8.

"**Y**ou shall not add unto the word which I command you, neither shall you diminish from it, that you may keep the Commandments of the L–rd your G–d which I command you."

Deuteronomy IV 2.

"**T**herefore shall you keep all the Commandments which I command you this day, that you may be strong and go in and possess the land, whither you go over to possess it.

And that you may prolong your days upon the land, which the L–rd swore unto your fathers to give unto them and their seed, a land flowing with milk and honey."

Deuteronomy XI 8–9.

1970

A birthday celebration

This book had its beginning at a birthday celebration. It was no ordinary birthday, neither was it celebrated in an ordinary fashion.

The celebration marked the eighty-first birthday of Shneur Zalman Shazar, President of Israel, and it took place on *Rosh Chodesh Kislev* 5731 (1970) at the Tzemach Tzedek *shul* in Jerusalem.

The Lubavitch Foundation of England took this opportunity to present a specially bound and inscribed copy of CHALLENGE[1] to the President.

A week later, in his office, President Shazar graciously received the representatives of the Lubavitch Foundation and remarked that in the intervening week he had browsed through CHALLENGE. He added that whilst he was most impressed with the book he had a major criticism: the section on "Chabad in Israel" was totally inadequate.

"Whilst I realise," said the President, "that even a whole book could not do complete justice to the theme, one article is certainly not enough. What about the wonderful pioneers of *Chabad* whose names have become a byword in the land; the schools, *yeshivos*, the spiritual and material work amongst the people of the land?" The President gesticulated dramatically

[1] An Encounter with Lubavitch-Chabad published by the Lubavitch Foundation of Great Britain 1970. An introduction to the history, philosophy and activities of the Chabad movement throughout the world.

and one could readily sense that without the cares of State he could easily write the book himself, drawing on his vast knowledge and memory of people and facts.

Imbued with the emotion and the need which the President so obviously portrayed, it was agreed that a supplement to CHALLENGE should be undertaken. The new volume would be devoted entirely to *Chabad* in Israel and as it would be of interest to people in many countries, it was decided that to obviate language difficulties it should be largely pictorial.

Right: President Shazar greets congregants at Tzemach Tzedek Shul on arrival for *shacharis* on the occasion of his 81st birthday.

Below: President Shazar being called to the Reading of the Law.

Above and below: Presentation of a
specially bound and inscribed copy
of CHALLENGE to President Shazar.

4   Now, over two years later, *Chabad in Israel* is completed and one has strong doubts as to its adequacy. Items may inadvertently have been omitted and important people may not have been mentioned. With the changing scene in Israel, particularly with the influx of Russian Jews, new institutions have been started, new activities have commenced, some of which may not appear in the following pages.

If the book is incomplete at the inception, what then is its purpose?

It is hoped that this supplement to CHALLENGE will portray something of the history of *Chabad* in the Holy Land and more particularly

Chabad's special contribution to its growth since 1948.

It seeks to show how a small group of men and women who, like all of us, have their personal lives to lead, families to bring up and livelihoods to earn, can devote themselves to sharing their spiritual wealth with other Jews and help them rediscover their natural and rightful heritage. It seeks to show how much can be achieved by a few; a few who are sure of their cause and fortified by a unique philosophy and teachings which have stood the test of time and of changing circumstances.

Pupils of Beth Chanah School with Mrs. Shazar (extreme left) at the President's birthday celebration.

6   This book is about a small army, many of them part-time amateurs who, under the direction of the Lubavitcher Rebbe שליט״א, are doing a very professional job and are, through their efforts, writing one of the great success stories of modern-day Israel.

Rabbi N. Sudak, Principal of the Lubavitch Foundation of Great Britain (second from right in lower illustration), and other representatives are received by President Shazar in his office.

Chabad in the
Holy Land

1777

First Chassidic Aliyah

Aliyah is not a new term in the vocabulary of *Chabad*. Veneration of the sanctity of the Land of Israel has an important place in *Chabad* teachings. The *Chassidic* community in the Holy Land will soon celebrate the 200th anniversary of the arrival of its first pilgrims in the Land of Our Forefathers.

It was in 1776, barely three years after the demise of Rabbi Dovber, the Maggid of Meseritch and the successor to the Baal Shem Tov, the founder of the *Chassidic* movement, that his leading disciples convened for the purpose of mapping the future course of the movement in the face of the crisis that had developed since his passing. Among the momentous decisions made at the conclave was one that set the stage for the first organised *Chassidic aliyah* under the leadership of the *Maggid*'s senior disciple Rabbi Menachem Mendel of Vitebsk and his two colleagues Rabbi Abraham of Kalisk and Rabbi Israel of Polotzk. The succession to the leadership of the movement in White Russia and Lithuania was unanimously bestowed upon Rabbi Shneur Zalman of Ladi, founder of the Lubavitch-Chabad movement.[1]

On the following *yahrzeit* of the *Maggid* (*Kislev* 19 5537—winter,

[1] See Nissan Mindel, *Rabbi Schneur Zalman of Liadi*, Kehot Publication Society, Brooklyn, N.Y. 1969, pp. 49f., 57f.

1776), a solemn gathering of his leading disciples met at the home of Rabbi Menachem Mendel in Horodok. The occasion was to serve also as a farewell to the *Chassidic* leaders before their departure for the Holy Land. A three-day conference was held to ensure the continuity and growth of the movement at home and the development of the *Chassidic* settlement in the Holy Land. The time of the emigration was set for the summer of that year (5537/1777).

Returning home to Liozna, Rabbi Shneur Zalman experienced a traumatic personal crisis. He felt a strong urge to join his colleagues and emigrate with them to the Holy Land, yet he was loath to abandon his responsibilities to his numerous followers and to his colleagues who depended on his financial support to the *Chassidic* group—about 300 strong—who were to settle in Palestine.

For three months he wrestled with this agonising problem. Finally, during *Chol-Hamoed Pesach*, he reached a decision. He informed his family and disciples that he would set out for the Holy Land immediately after *Pesach*.

In the beginning of the month of *Iyar*, Rabbi Shneur Zalman with his family, accompanied by his brothers and their families and some senior disciples, left Liozna. They made their way, unhurriedly, to Mohilev, on the Dniester River.

On the way, Rabbi Shneur Zalman tarried in various towns in the districts of Podolia and Volhynia, taking leave of his many followers with parting lectures and sermons.

When he finally arrived in Mohilev, his senior colleagues Rabbi Menachem Mendel and Rabbi Abraham, who had preceded him, did not disguise their displeasure at his intention to relinquish the position which had been bestowed upon him. During the next three weeks Rabbi Shneur Zalman and his colleagues spent many hours daily in profound discussions. When they left, the *Alter Rebbe* remained in Mohilev for two more weeks which he spent in seclusion. Then he let it be known that he would return to Lithuania.

Rabbi Shneur Zalman eventually returned to Liozna and took the reins of leadership of the *Chassidic* movement firmly in his hands.

In the meantime, the first *Chassidic* émigrés arrived in the Holy Land on *Elul* 5, 5537 (1777) and settled in Safed and Tveriah (Tiberias).

Rabbi Shneur Zalman made it one of his primary concerns to raise funds for the support of the fledgling *Chassidic* settlement in the Holy Land. In every *Chassidic* community he appointed a special local representative to be in charge of collecting contributions for this cause. At least once a year he sent out personal emissaries to visit those communities. They were eagerly welcomed for they brought the Rebbe's teachings, inspiration and blessings to distant communities and returned with lists of contributors and their contributions.

For years Rabbi Shneur Zalman sent huge sums of money for the support of the *Chassidic* families and institutions in the Holy Land. In 1788 he founded the Kolel Chabad, an umbrella organisation for *Chabad* institutions and needy families in Palestine. It was the recipient and distributor of the funds which were regularly sent by him. This organisation is still in existence and carries out its functions as of old, only on a much larger scale.

[1] The history of the portrait reproduced here may be found in *CHALLENGE – an encounter with Lubavitch-Chabad,* page 24.

Rabbi Shneur Zalman of Ladi.[1]

שניאור זלמן בהרב מוהר ברוך נבג"מ זיע"א בעל המחבר ספר התניא והשו"ע ולקוטי תורה

From time to time Rabbi Shneur Zalman sent out pastoral letters to his faithful to keep the remembrance and love of the Holy Land burning in their hearts. In one such epistle he writes:

. . . To arouse the ancient love and fondness for our Holy Land that it burn like glowing embers from the inmost of man and a profound heart . . . that everyone give generously and in a consistently growing measure from year to year, in accordance with the [Divine] attribute of Supernal Holiness which irradiates the Holy Land with a light that is constantly renewed and increased, as it is written: "Forever are the eyes of the L–rd your G–d upon it, from the beginning of the year to the end of the year."[1]

Rabbi Shneur Zalman's devotion to the *Chassidic* community in Palestine and the financial support which he sent it regularly later served, as a result of reckless calumny by the opponents of the *Chassidic* movement, as the basis of serious charges against him of high treason and subversive activities. At that time Palestine was under Turkish rule and Russia and Turkey were in a state of war. In 1798 Rabbi Shneur Zalman was arrested on charges of helping the war effort of Turkey against Russia, it being alleged that in return he would be recognised as King of the Jews in a Jewish State in Palestine under Turkey's protection. The absurdity of the charges soon emerged and the *Chassidic* leader was completely exonerated, giving rise to the great *Chassidic* festival of *Yud tes Kislev*, the anniversary of his liberation.[2]

It is interesting to note that in so far as Rabbi Shneur Zalman was concerned, far from regarding his activity on behalf of the *Chassidic* community in the Holy Land as the cause of his arrest and suffering, he saw in it the very reason for his release and victory over his adversaries. This he expresses in his letters to two other *Chassidic* leaders, Rabbi Levi Yitzchak of Berditchev and Rabbi Baruch of Mezibush:

It was from G–d to grant us the zechus [*merit*], *for the sake of the Holy Land and its inhabitants, and this is what stood us in good stead and will continue to do so on every occasion in the future, to bring us deliverance, relief and expansion in times of distress, and raise our honour in the glory of G–d. . . .*

The *Chassidic* settlements in Safed and Tiberias gradually grew and expanded. Other *Chassidic* families settled there with the encouragement and support of Rabbi Shneur Zalman, the *Alter Rebbe* as he is reverently called by *Chabad Chassidim*.

After Rabbi Menachem Mendel died (1788), Rabbi Abraham of Kalisk remained the sole leader of the *Chassidic* community in the Holy Land. Rabbi Shneur Zalman continued to serve as patron and benefactor to the *Chassidim* in Palestine until the end of his days (1812).

[1] Chapter XIV, *Igereth Hakodesh* (part IV of *Tanya*), tr. by Rabbi J. I. Schochet, KPS, 1968. The quotation has been simplified here.

[2] N. Mindel, op. cit., ch. X.

The leadership of the *Chabad Chassidim* passed from the *Alter Rebbe* to his son Rabbi Dovber, the *Mittler Rebbe*, who continued his illustrious father's work with equal dedication. Having made his residence in Lubavitch (White Russia), not far from Ladi, the *Chabad Chassidim* were soon to become more popularly known as "Lubavitcher" *Chassidim*, after the name of the "Town of Love" which served as the centre of the movement for over a century (until the outbreak of World War I in 1914).

For various reasons the *Mittler Rebbe* decided that it would be in the interests of the *Chassidic* community in the Holy Land for it to be concentrated in Hebron, the City of Our Patriarchs. Accordingly, he urged the *Chassidim* of Safed and Tiberias to move to Hebron. At least fifteen families immediately responded to his call and moved as a group from Safed to Hebron.

In an encyclical to his followers (dated 5583/1823), in which he appealed for redoubled efforts to support the *Chassidic* community and institutions in Hebron, he emphasised the holiness of the City of Our Patriarchs and the special *zechus* of supporting the *yeshivah* there.

The *Mittler Rebbe* urged his followers to acquire land in Hebron. He himself bought a piece of property in that city, on which stood an old synagogue known as the "Synagogue of Our Father Abraham".

Left: Bimah at "Synagogue of Our Father Abraham", Hebron.

Opposite: Chabad Yeshivah, Hebron. Drawing by Baruch Nachshon.

יעקב מרחוק אתה וירושלם תעלה על לבבם

הסכת ושמע ישראל אחינו מרחמינו ויהי ישרון עם קדוש עם קדושי עליון אוהבי ה' ירך לבבכם מקהל עדת קדושה אשר נעשה אמרידם
בארין הקדושה באם אנים לשיראל ההרים וקול להרים כשר לא מצרת תמעלים משדשו כבי עקב על פתחי נדיבות אחינו
מארצי בכיר נלשי בשבר לבמי בדמין שעמו בער ריתונו בחשכת הארין ובאה שיריכם נדשק כלהיתוכם
חני נא אזניכם שימו לבבכם ותח נפשכם וישבעת אליכם כמשח קדש כן השבים :

אהבי ה' ... **נין**

נדבה ...

נצרים אלכסנדרי נא אמון ... **מערב החיצון**
יוהרן ... **מערב הפנימי** ... **ירושלם**

קול ... **כהל המערב** ... **חברון** מערת המכפלה

שי הנה אנחנו בקרש ...

ותה ... **חברון וירושלם**

הרב חק בארן ... **אבנם** ... **קול הזריה הזבה**

בסערות ... **ואשר** ... **עתה** ...

ותשבר ...

ובכל ... **שאול אשכנזי** ... **תרומתה** ... **ירושלם**

ועתה ... **פקוח נפשות ירושלם**

נבודרי ... **אנחנו** ... **שלום**

Thus the *Chabad* colony in Hebron grew steadily. It was the only *Ashkenazi* community there. Prominent *Chassidim* who came to settle in Hebron bolstered the colony. Among the newcomers was Rabbi Yaacov Slonim, son-in-law of the *Mittler Rebbe*, who brought his family with him. His wife, the Rebbetzin Menuchah Rachel, who survived her husband, was long remembered as the matriarch and "grandmother" of the community. Many of the *Chassidic* families in Hebron were her descendants. When leading *Chassidim* from Jerusalem and other places visited Hebron, their first call was to pay their respects to this Grand Old Lady.

The settlement of the *Chassidim* in Hebron brought new vitality to the local *Sephardi* community which existed there before their arrival.

Tomb of Isaac, Hebron. Drawing by Baruch Nachshon.

However, it did not serve to lessen the hostility of their Arab neighbours. Several years after the arrival of the first *Chassidim* in Hebron, a rebellion broke out in Jerusalem against the central Turkish government. The surrounding country, including Hebron, was thrown into turmoil and the central government had great difficulty in restoring order in that part of Palestine. Powerful Arab sheikhs in the area took advantage of the situation to oppress the Jews and extort money from them. In addition, marauding Druse bands often swept down from the hills to plunder and pillage the defenceless Jews.

The position of the *Ashkenazi* Jews in Hebron was even worse than that of the oriental or *Sephardi* Jews. The latter, having lived among the Arabs for decades, speaking Arabic and experienced in dealings with their hostile neighbours, could cope a little better with the circumstances. Not so the newly arrived Jews from Russia, who were the victims of relentless harassment and extortion by local Arab effendis. Historical records of those days speak of a particularly ruthless sheikh of the village of Dura who terrorised Hebron and its environs. He considered the Jews of Hebron as his personal subjects and property and in return for the protection he gave them against attacks by marauders he exacted a hard price through exorbitant taxes and levies. He regarded himself

Top left: Seal of Yeshivah Chassdei Avos. Under auspices of *Chabad*, Hebron, 1909.

Above: Letter heading of Toras Emes Yeshivah, Hebron, 1913.

Below left: Seal of *Chabad* community, Hebron 1866; outside circle reads "Kiryat Arba that is Hebron" and enumerates the Patriarchs and Matriarchs and Adam and Eve buried at Machpelah—pictured in centre of seal.

as absolute master of the Jews and their belongings, coming and going in and out of their homes at his will and whim. If he saw anything he wanted among their possessions he simply took it or even ordered the Jewish owner to bring it to him.

The Turkish authorities were reluctant or incapable of doing anything to put an end to this oppression of the Jews and the Jews had no recourse except to pay off the Arab sheikhs. Thus, when the Kolel money arrived, a part of it had to be set aside for ransom money. For a long time this item appeared on the books of the Kolel as a payment to the "Black Rabbi", who was none other than the Sheikh of Dura.

The oppression of the Hebron Jews by the Arabs united the *Sephardi* and *Ashkenazi* Jews. They joined to bring their plight to the attention of their brethren abroad. As a result, too, the two communities co-operated in local efforts to improve their situation and they established joint communal institutions.

As the needs of the *Chabad Yeshivah* and other institutions grew, the *Mittler Rebbe* intensified his fund-raising efforts. Virtually every *Chassidic* family had a charity box bearing the inscription "Tzedakah of Rabbi Meir Baal Haness" for the support of the needy in the Holy Land. Emissaries and collectors paid regular visits to the homes of the *Chassidim* to collect the funds which the *Mittler Rebbe* then transmitted to the Kolel Chabad for distribution. Since there was no direct postal service with Hebron, an office of Kolel Chabad was established in Jerusalem which in turn sent the funds to Hebron.

The establishment of the Kolel branch in Jerusalem was the beginning of a new *Chassidic* colony in the Old City. The nucleus of *Chassidic* families there expanded and in due course they had their own synagogue built in 1848. The street where the synagogue and *Chassidic* dwellings were located became known as Chabad Street, even among the Arabs.

According to a letter written in 1867 by Shimon Chaikin, one of the early settlers in Hebron (in which he states his age as ninety), the *Chabad* community in the City of the Patriarchs then numbered 400 persons.

Prominent *Chassidic* Rabbis stood at the head of the Hebron Community in its early period and for about seventy years its spiritual leader was Rabbi Shimon Menashe. He came to the Holy Land at the age of six with his father who settled in Safed and when the *Chabad Chassidim* began to move to Hebron his father resettled there. The young Shimon Menashe excelled in his *Torah* studies. Later, he took up house painting as his trade and before *Pesach* it was his job to repaint and whitewash the houses and rooms of the local residents. The modest income from this work sustained him for the rest of the year, which he devoted to the study of *Torah* and *Chassidus*. He gave up this occupation when he was elected Rabbi.

He distinguished himself not only as an outstanding *Torah* scholar, but also as a public servant. Anyone in need always found in him an attentive and warm friend and no person was turned away by him empty-handed. Whether the need was for a garment or for *Shabbos* provisions and the like, the Rabbi would write a special "note" to the treasurer of Kolel Chabad for an appropriate contribution. Before long, the treasury was exhausted and large debts were incurred. Rabbi Shimon Menashe was impelled to make the long and arduous journey to Lubavitch in Russia. The then Lubavitcher Rebbe, the *Tzemach Tzedek*, received him with honour and affection. Rabbi Shimon Menashe returned to the Holy Land not only with sufficient funds to repay all the debts of the Kolel in Hebron and Jerusalem but with a surplus to provide for future needs.

In due course, some members of the *Chassidic* community in Hebron entered into matrimonial ties with families in Jaffa. Thus the *Chabad* influence made itself felt there and it was not long before a *Chabad* community began to flourish also in Jaffa. The members here were largely merchants who contributed in no small measure to the economic and spiritual development of the local community. The *Chabad* community itself soon reached the point when it required its own Rabbi and spiritual leader. Their choice was the prominent *Chassid* Rabbi Shneur Slonim, a grandson of Rebbetzin Menuchah Rachel, daughter of the *Mittler Rebbe*. In this respect, the *Chabad* community in Jaffa outpaced the *Chabad* community in Jerusalem which could not yet boast its own *Chabad* Rabbi.

The *Chabad* communities in Jaffa and Jerusalem grew at the expense of the one in Hebron, yet the City of Our Patriarchs continued to be favoured by the Lubavitcher Rebbes. The *Tzemach Tzedek* like his predecessor, his father-in-law the *Mittler Rebbe*, encouraged a number of *Chassidim* to settle in Hebron. Among them was the Kazarnovsky family, related to the *Mittler Rebbe*, who settled in Hebron in 1861, and Shlomo Zalman Klonsky who also brought his grandchildren with him.

A closer personal contact was established between Hebron and Lubavitch with occasional visits by *Chassidim* from Hebron to Lubavitch to spend some time with their Rebbe. The sons of the Rebbetzin Menuchah Rachel visited Lubavitch several times and were received by the Rebbe with distinct honour. Emissaries from Hebron sometimes travelled abroad to help the fund-raising efforts.

Succeeding generations of *Chabad* leadership, the Rebbe *MaHaRaSh*

Opposite: Ruins of Jewish Quarter, Hebron.

(Rabbi Shmuel) and the Rebbe *RaShaB* (Rabbi Sholom Dovber), continued to devote a great deal of attention to the *Chassidic* communities, especially in Hebron and Jerusalem. In 1912 the Hebron community received great stimulus when the *RaShaB* sent a group of selected students, headed by Rabbi Shlomo Zalman Havlin, to establish a *yeshivah* there. The *yeshivah*, named "Toras Emes", was built on Rabbi Sholom Dovber's own property in Hebron and it became a centre of *Torah* and *Chassidus* in the Holy Land.[1] It became known throughout the *Yishuv* and attracted gifted students from all parts of the land.

[1] It was modelled on the Yeshivah Tomchei Tmimim which the Rebbe *RaShaB* had established in Lubavitch in 1897.

Below: Hebron, desecrated remains of Avrohom Avinu Synagogue.

Opposite: Martyrs Section, Hebron.

Unfortunately, just as the Hebron community began to flourish with renewed vigour, World War I broke out. The financial basis of the *yeshivah* was shattered since the funds from Russia, the source of its support, ceased. The *yeshivah* students scattered and many of them were forced to leave the country as citizens of an enemy State. The disruption of the *yeshivah* was a hard blow for the entire *Chassidic* community of Hebron.

After the war, and under the leadership of the late Lubavitcher Rebbe, Rabbi Joseph Isaac Schneersohn, the Yeshivah Toras Emes was revived in Hebron and once again it and the entire Hebron community flourished. The Arab massacre in 1929 brought this era to a tragic end. The *yeshivah* then moved to Jerusalem where it continues to grow in numbers and in influence.

Above: Chabad Yeshivah, Hebron, now converted to
Moslem School (*below*).

JERUSALEM

The history of the early *Chabad* settlement in Jerusalem[1] went through three stages of development. It began with individual *Chassidic* families who settled there. Among them was Rabbi Chaim Moiseef, the first *shochet* of the *Ashkenazi* community, who came to the Holy Land with the first *Chassidic aliyah* in 1777. Amongst the early *Chassidic* settlers in Jerusalem was also Rabbi Yaacov Slonim, son-in-law of the *Mittler Rebbe*, who first lived in Hebron and towards the end of his life moved to Jerusalem. During this early stage, the number of *Chabad Chassidim* in the Holy City was small and they had no organised community of their own.

During the next phase (1841–1855) the *Chabad* settlement in Jerusalem made notable strides. In 1847 the renowned *Gaon* and *Chassid* Rabbi Eliyahu Yosef Rivlin, author of *Oholey Yosef*, emigrated to Jerusalem with the blessing of the *Tzemach Tzedek*. He established the first *Chabad* synagogue in Jerusalem and was revered for his saintliness and *Talmudic* scholarship. His influence was greatly felt throughout the Jewish community in the Holy City and extended also to Hebron, which he visited frequently and where he gave *Talmudic* lectures.

During those years a number of *Chabad* families moved from Hebron to Jerusalem. They concentrated in two streets in the Old City, later to be known as Baron Street and Chabad Street, which formed a part of a thriving Jewish Quarter until it was overrun and destroyed by the Arab Legion in 1948.

Among the prominent *Chabad* families that settled there were those of Rabbi Shneur Zalman Schneerson, Rabbi Yaacov Zevulun Moiseef and Rabbi Chaim Schmerling. Another prominent newcomer to Jerusalem in those days was Rabbi Uri Orenstein, one of the *Tzemach Tzedek*'s *Chassidim*, who emigrated to Palestine in 1831 and settled at first in Safed, then Hebron and finally made his home in the Holy City. He served as an emissary of the *Chabad Chassidim* of Jerusalem and Hebron for fund-raising purposes and visited the *Tzemach Tzedek* in Lubavitch. Upon his return he was appointed treasurer and administrator of the Kolel Chabad. Other heads of the Kolel during that period were Rabbi Shlomo Epstein and Rabbi S. N. Schneerson. In 1855, out of the several hundred *Ashkenazi* Jews in Jerusalem, Kolel Chabad had fifty members. In that year the various *Chassidic* groups formed a *Beth Din* of their own with Rabbi Menachem Nachum of Polotzk, the Rabbi and spiritual leader of the *Chabad Chassidim*, as one of its members.

This period also saw the arrival of the venerable *Gaon* and Chief Rabbi of Bobroysk, Rabbi Baruch Mordechai, one of the *Alter Rebbe*'s

[1] The later development of *Chabad* in Jerusalem is dealt with on page 96.

Chassidim. Prior to his departure for the Holy Land in 1851, he spent several months with the *Tzemach Tzedek* in Lubavitch. He was about ninety years old when he came to Jerusalem and died within the year of his arrival.

The third phase in the development of the *Chabad* community in Jerusalem began after 1855 by when it had become fully organised with its own newly built synagogue.

In that year, too, Rabbi Eliyahu Yosef Rivlin paid a visit to the *Tzemach Tzedek*, bringing a personal report of the *Chabad Chassidim* in the Holy Land. Apparently he utilised his visit also for the purpose of raising additional funds for the *Chabad* communities in Jerusalem and Hebron.

Above: A letter from General Committee of United Jewish Community, Hebron, 1918; Joint President, Rabbi J. J. Slonim.

Right: Chabad student as pictured in *The Book of Jerusalem*, published in 1918.

Left: Anglo Palestine Bank, Hebron, 1913. Standing extreme right, Bank Treasurer Yosef Rivlin. Seated, Area Treasurer Alter Rivlin (Jerusalem), Dr. Leventin, Menachem Slonim.

Below: Historical photograph of four generations of Slonim family, descendants of Rebbetzin Menuchah Rachel Slonim, daughter of the *Mittler Rebbe.*

During the leadership of the *Tzemach Tzedek* a new *Chabad* community was established in Safed. Most of these immigrants came from Rumania, where a large *Chabad* community flourished under the influence of Rabbi Yitzchak Moshe of Yassi, a disciple of the *Alter Rebbe*. Apparently the *Tzemach Tzedek* encouraged many of the *Chabad Chassidim* in Rumania to emigrate to the Holy Land and at his suggestion they settled in Safed. Among the new settlers there were Rabbi Berl the *shochet*, Rabbi Velvel Tzipres and Beila, a niece of the *Tzemach Tzedek*. She had grown up in his house and had married a prominent *Chassid*, Rabbi Yeshaya

Above: Rabbi Yaacov Yosef Slonim, seated front row extreme left, at meeting with British Government officials and Arabs, Hebron, 1920.

Left: Licence given to A. D. Slonim to carry a firearm, Hebron 1929.

Right: Shloime Slonim, sole survivor of his family following the Hebron Massacre, 1929.

Hurwitz. When she was widowed, the *Tzemach Tzedek* arranged
emigration to Safed together with her family, whom he supported
gular subvention. Records indicate that there were visits by large
of *Chabad Chassidim* from Safed to Lubavitch to be with their
the *Tzemach Tzedek*.

ng the *Tzemach Tzedek*'s disciples who emigrated to the Holy
after his demise were Rabbi Shneur Zalman, author of *Toras
who was the spiritual leader of the *Chassidim* in Jerusalem and
Moshe Meshel Gelbstein.

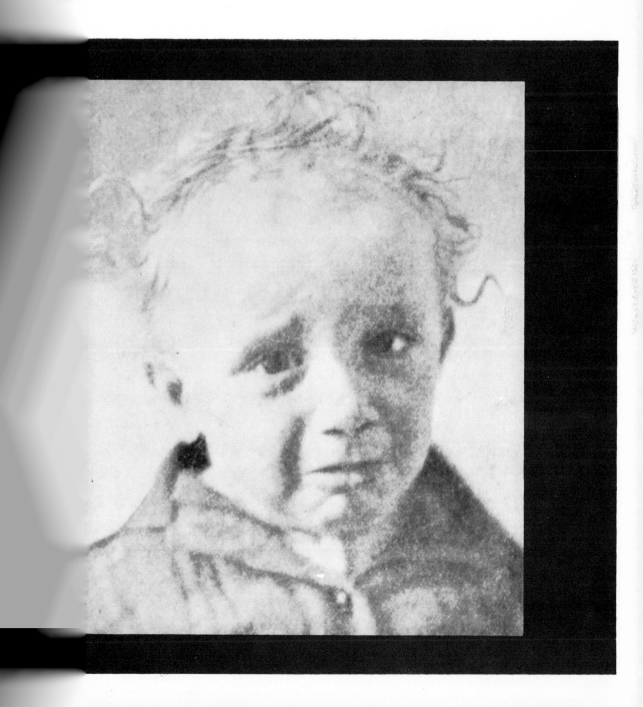

תוכני **ירושלם** תובב"א

שנת וֵֿאֵצֵֿמֵֿ֒ח קֶרֶן לְדֹוֵֿד עַבֵֿדֵ֒י לפֵ"ק

בְרוך אתה בבואך
בוא ברוך ה'!

פתחו שערים ויבא גוי צדיק בן צדיק שְׁנָיִם!

מה נאוו על ההרים רגלי מבשר, משמיע שלום אומד לציון הנה הַשר **משה מונטיפיורי**
הי"ו, יבֹא שעריך, לשְֹחֵל כטוֹב שוֹכֵי חדריך, ומתגורריס בצעריך.

את בת **ירושלם** שֶלֵי עִנִי ואָתָן לבוֹשֵׁך שָנֵי, הנה שר וגדול אֵן וֹאֹשֹ אֹנֵ אֹ יֹדֹריֹ הֹיֹס
על מפתן שעריך, — י ואתה יושבי ירושלם עברים הֵשֹבֵֿריֹס כֹראֹֹשֹ עֹם הֵקֹֹם
חֹגֹֹרוֹ מֹתֹניֹכֹם, וֹיֹגֵל שֹמֹחֹתֹכֹם, וֹֹקֹומֹוֹ קֹֹרֹמֹוֹ אֹֹת פֹֹנֹ הֹֹֹֹשֹֹֹר לֹֹֹֹֹֹֹם טֹֹֹֹֹֹֹֹֹֹס כֹֹאֹֹֹֹֹֹֹבֹֹס, וֹֹֹֹֹֹֹֹֹֹֹֹֹ אֹֹֹת קֹֹֹֹֹֹל
בֹֹֹֹֹֹֹֹֹֹֹֹֹֹֹם, בֹֹֹֹֹֹֹֹֹֹֹֹֹֹֹֹֹֹֹֹ וֹֹֹֹֹֹֹֹֹֹֹֹֹֹֹֹֹֹ אֹֹֹֹֹֹה, וֹֹֹֹֹֹֹֹֹֹֹֹֹֹֹֹֹֹֹֹֹֹֹֹ פֹֹֹֹֹ ה' בֹֹֹֹֹ גֹֹֹֹֹֹֹת יֹֹֹֹֹֹֹֹל,
וֹכֹֹֹֹֹר שֹֹֹֹֹֹם יֹֹֹֹֹֹֹֹם אֹֹֹֹֹֹֹֹֹבֹֹֹֹֹֹ זֹה, וֹֹֹֹֹֹן תֹֹֹֹֹֹֹֹֹ לֹֹֹֹֹֹֹֹֹֹת בֹֹֹֹֹֹֹֹֹֹֹ פֹֹֹֹ מֹֹֹֹֹ לֹֹֹֹֹֹֹן בֹֹֹֹֹֹֹֹֹֹֹ בֹֹֹֹֹֹֹֹֹ אֹֹֹֹֹֹן!

בֹֹֹן הֹֹֹֹֹֹֹֹֹֹֹ הֹֹֹֹֹֹֹֹֹֹֹ בֹֹֹֹֹ גֹֹם קֹֹֹֹֹֹ רֹֹֹֹֹ וֹֹֹֹֹֹֹ בֹֹ קֹֹֹֹ כֹֹֹל חֹֹֹֹֹ **חב"ד** יֹֹֹֹֹ עֹֹֹֹֹֹ
ירושלם תֹֹֹ, לֹֹֹֹֹ פֹֹֹ חֹֹֹֹֹֹ בֹֹֹֹֹֹֹֹ, וֹֹֹֹל תֹֹֹֹ לֹֹ' שֹֹֹֹֹֹ, וֹֹֹֹֹ וֹֹֹֹֹ אֹֹֹ
אֹֹֹ הֹֹֹֹן הֹֹֹֹֹ לֹֹֹֹֹֹ עֹֹֹ לֹֹֹֹ אֹֹֹֹֹ אֹֹ אֹֹֹֹֹ, וֹֹֹֹֹֹֹ, וֹֹֹֹֹֹ טֹֹֹ, יֹֹֹֹ לֹֹֹֹ, וֹֹֹֹֹֹֹ בֹֹֹֹֹ, עֹֹ
26 פֹֹֹֹֹֹֹֹ לֹֹֹֹ! — י וֹֹֹֹן בֹֹֹֹֹ עֹֹ הֹֹֹֹֹ כֹֹֹֹֹֹֹ רֹֹֹ וֹֹֹל תֹֹֹֹ וֹֹֹֹֹ!

נֹֹֹֹֹ, אֹֹֹֹֹֹ שֹֹֹֹֹֹ

נֹֹֹֹֹ, אֹֹֹל לֹֹֹֹ
נֹֹֹֹֹ אֹֹֹ אֹֹֹֹֹֹ, הֹֹֹ

CHABAD INSTITUTIONS IN HEBRON

1. *SYNAGOGUES*

[1] This survey was
the third made in a
period of twenty
years. The first two
were made in 1855
and 1866.

In 5615 (1855) the *Chabad* community consisted of 142 persons, among
them 44 men, who congregated in two synagogues. The first, known
as "The Large Synagogue", was bought by Rabbi Yecheskel Menasheh.
The *Beth Din* consisted of Rabbi Avrohom Dov, Rabbi Nochum Arye
and Rabbi Shimon Menashe who was the senior member of the *Beth Din*.
He also acted as treasurer of the community. The *gabbai* was Rabbi
Yaacov Slonim. There was no official *chazan* and on Holy Days Rabbi
Shimon Menashe, Rabbi Yaacov Slonim and Rabbi Leib Slonim
officiated. The *baal korah* was Rav Levi Yitzchok Slonim and the
shamash was Reb Zalman Cohen. The *sofer* was Reb Dovid Cohen. There
was a *mikvah* in the basement of the *shul*.

The second, known as "The Small Synagogue", was situated close to
the *Sephardi* synagogue and had been purchased by the *Mittler Rebbe*.
The officials of the larger synagogue also governed the affairs of this
synagogue which had a small *mikvah* for women.

In 5626 (1866) the community consisted of 228 persons, including
61 men. There was now a *yeshivah* attached to "The Small Synagogue".
The community had two *mikvaos*, one hot and one cold.

By 5635 (1875) the *Chabad* community has greatly increased to 489
persons, including 140 men. The two synagogues have assumed proper
names; the larger synagogue is called "Beis Menachem" and the other
"Ohel Avrohom".

2. *BATEI MEDRASHIM*

In 5615 (1855) there was one *Beis Hamedrash* which was situated next
to "The Large Synagogue" and known as "Das Moshe V'Yehudis"
(Montefiore). The *Rosh Yeshivah* was Rabbi Shimon Menashe and there
were eighteen pupils. Study started one hour after *shacharis* and continued, with breaks for *mincha* and *maariv*, until midnight. The pupils
learned *mishnayos* with its commentaries; *Gemorrah* with all the commentaries; *Agadeta* and *Mussar*; *Poskim*, *Zohar* and *Raishis Chochmah*. *Kabbalah*
was taught by Rabbi Yaacov Slonim as were matters pertaining to the
weekly *Sidra*.

In 5626 (1866) there were three *Batei Medrashim*. The *yeshivah* "Das
Moshe V'Yehudis" had moved into "The Large Synagogue" and had
fifteen pupils. The *yeshivah* "Talmud u Poskim" was situated in the

loft of the same synagogue and had ten students. The third was called "Chevra Shas Al Pi Admur Shlito". The pupils studied in their own homes, each having been assigned a different *mesechta* of *Shas* so that collectively the entire *Shas* would be learned each year. The *Siyum* to mark the completion of the *Shas* was held each year on the 19th *Kislev*. Of the pupils attending the *yeshivos* some learned before midnight and some after midnight. Rabbi Shimon Menashe was the *Rosh Yeshivos*, holding this position in an honorary capacity.

By 5635 (1875) the three *Batei Medrashim* have amalgamated into two. The first is now called Beis Menachem, the same name as the *shul* itself. Rabbi Shimon Menashe continues as the Dean and the pupils, who learn three *shiurim* a day, are all the *talmidei chachomim* who *daven* in the *shul*. The second is now known as the Beis Hamedrash Haketanoh Ohel Avrohom after the smaller synagogue. Rabbi Nochum Arye is the Honorary Dean. The pupils, who learn two *shiurim* a day, are all the *talmidei chachomim* who *daven* in this *shul*.

3. SCHOOLS

Children are taught *Tenach*, *Gemorrah* and commentaries at the homes of the teachers. The teachers are paid partly by the parents and partly by the community.

4. SOCIETIES

In 5615 (1855) there were four societies in this *Chabad* community. By 5635 (1875) in line with the general increase of numbers in the community the number of societies has grown to seven:

(a) *Bikur Cholim*

Its function is to cater for the needs of and to provide assistance for the sick. It is headed by Rabbi Leib Slonim. Amongst its functions as listed in its constitution is to decide whether to transfer the sick to Jerusalem or to bring a doctor from there, and to stock the various medicines most commonly needed. The funds for this society are raised by voluntary contributions and by offerings made at *Yomim Tovim* by those called to the Reading of the Law. Sir Moses Montefiore contributes £5 a year to this society.

(b) *Chevra Kadisha*

All members of the community make up the membership of this society. The members officiate, where necessary, according to lots, and their duties are all matters pertaining to the burial and honour of the dead. It is under the direction of Rabbi Levi Yitzchok Slonim.

(c) *Hachnossas Kalloh*

Its function is to assist the poor and orphaned in their marriage preparations, including the provision of dowries. This committee is led by Rabbi Zalman Fundaminsky who has authority to give assistance up to a specified amount, above which the consent of other members of the society is required. Sir Moses Montefiore contributes £5 a year towards the funds of this society, the balance being raised by door-to-door collections.

(d) *Olei Regolim*

This society is headed by Rabbi Zalman Slonim and its purpose is to ensure that ten members of the community go to Jerusalem each *Yom Tov* to pray there for peace on behalf of our brethren in the Diaspora. Each of the ten is given two pounds towards his travelling expenses. Ten different people drawn by lots go on each occasion and as the purpose is to fulfil a *mitzvah* this special fund has been established. The fund is provided by a levy on all members of the community and any deficiency is met by the Kolel Chabad.

(e) *Hachnossas Orchim*

This society is under the leadership of Rabbi Eliezer Shimon Kosroff. Its function is to provide hospitality (food, board and lodgings) to all those who come from afar to pray at the holy resting places of our Forefathers. It is stipulated that at every pilgrimage the leader of this society is to greet and meet the visitors, to ascertain their needs and to make every effort to accommodate them for three days. The funds are raised by various means and it would also appear that there is a city tax on all members of *Chabad* so that they should merit being known as *Bnei Avrohom Avinu* who was the foremost *machnes orach*.

(f) *Chevra Linno*

The function of this society is for people to visit and stay overnight in the house of a sick person to cater for his needs. Two people are sent each night to stay with the invalid during the course of his illness.

(g) *Chevras Gemillas Chasodim*

Under the leadership of Rabbi Benjamin Rivlin, this society has as its purpose "the granting of loans to the poor in the time of their pressure".

1929 An Historic Visit

[1] Extracts from a diary of this visit appear on pages 33 to 50.

In *Tammuz* 5689 (1929), a few weeks before the massacres in Hebron, the late Lubavitcher Rebbe, Rabbi Joseph Isaac Schneersohn, arrived in the Holy Land[1] where he visited Hebron.

Special permits for three people to accompany the Rebbe and his party were obtained for the occasion. The general arrangements for the Rebbe's visit to *Eretz Yisroel* had been made by Rabbi Eliezer Dan Slonim who also took responsibility for the Rebbe's visit to the Cave of Machpelah and the other Holy Places. Entry to the mosque over the Cave of Machpelah was normally forbidden to Jews and also to Christians, but on this occasion Rabbi Slonim succeeded in obtaining special permits to enter.

On his arrival, the Rebbe was greeted and accompanied into the City of Hebron by representatives of all sectors of the Jewish community, including students of the Slobodka Yeshivah in Hebron.

The plan of the tour was that the visiting party should enter the cave by way of "Jacob's Gate"—which was normally forbidden to Jews—and leave by way of "Abraham's Gate", the famous entrance with the "seven steps" which Jews were permitted to use.

At Jacob's Gate, the Rebbe and his party, comprising his son-in-law Rabbi Shmaryahu Gurary, Rabbi Jacob Joseph Slonim, Rabbi Eliezer Dan Slonim, Rabbi Israel Dobrutz, Rabbi Yitzchok Dobrutz and Rabbi Shneur Zalman Klonsky, were greeted by Arab notables. The visitors were given special leather sandals so that they should not be forced to remove their shoes as was the formal custom.

The party entered the place of the graves of the Patriarchs, Arab guides explaining the location of each grave. They were shown the pit next to the headstone of Abraham and Sarah, below which burned an eternal oil-lamp. The Rebbe, who led the group, appeared totally absorbed in thought, eyes closed, lips moving all the time. One observer remarked that the Rebbe seemed totally familiar with every path in the cave as if it was his own home. The visit passed without even a whisper being exchanged.

The excitement continued until they reached the "Gate of Abraham"; the party then commenced to descend the numerous steps until they reached the seventh—which was as far as Jews were permitted to descend.

An historic visit was at an end.

Translation of extracts from a diary kept by
Rabbi Shimon Glitzenstein of the visit to
the Holy Land by the late Lubavitcher
Rebbe, Rabbi Joseph Isaac Schneersohn in
Tammuz/Av 5689 (1929)

Thursday 17th Tammuz 5689 (1929)

We received today the good news of the impending visit of the Rebbe Shlito to Eretz Yisroel.

In the letter informing us of his visit, the Rebbe stresses the main purpose of his coming to Eretz Yisroel *at this time. The text of the Rebbe's letter is reproduced below:*

Monday First day Rosh Chodesh Tammuz *5689*

Riga

Yeshivas Toras Emes,
Headed by the Rabbis and Chassidim,
the Menahelim *and Principals of*
the Yeshivos, *G–d bless them,*
in the Holy City of Jerusalem,
may it be speedily rebuilt.

Greetings and Blessings,

In the country of my birth I was accustomed to visit from time to time the Holy resting places of my Holy forbears, our Rebbes of blessed memory, to pray there and to awaken great mercy for ourselves, our talmidim *and* Anash *together with all our brethren, may they live long. I am at present precluded from travelling to the country of my birth and I have decided, with the help of G–d, to make the journey to our Holy Land, may it be speedily rebuilt, to visit the Holy places there.*

I had been unable to finalise my travel plans until I had ascertained what documents and permits were required by law. I have today received information together with all the necessary permits and documents and I am now able to advise you that, with G–d's help, I will start the journey together with my son-in-law, Rabbi Shmaryahu Gurary, on Tuesday 22nd Tammuz *through Brindisi on the boat which leaves on Sunday for Alexandria.*

I think that the duration of our stay in the Holy Land will be two weeks. During that time I want, with G–d's help, to visit different places. I will plan my itinerary on arrival.

With blessings,

(signed)

The good news contained in this letter has brought great joy to Orthodox Jewry in the Holy Land and especially to Chabad circles. Everyone awaits the Rebbe's arrival with great excitement.

The Rebbe's intended visit has aroused a special interest. It is well known that all the Chabad Rebbes had a strong desire to go to Eretz Yisroel and were prevented by extraordinary obstacles such as those which caused the Alter Rebbe to cancel his journey when he was already en route. The work for the Holy Land initiated and executed by the holy chain of Chabad Rebbes and especially the great work of the Rebbe for Orthodox Jewry is well known. Because the Rebbe transcends parties and movements, all sections of Jewry in Eretz Yisroel have commenced preparations to receive him. His reputation—his efforts for the continuance of Judaism, elevating Torah and mitzvos through great self sacrifice—is such that everyone realises that it is their duty to receive this exceptional person with appropriate honour. The Chief Rabbi of Eretz Yisroel, the Ashkenazi community in Jerusalem and the Central Committee of Agudas Yisroel in Eretz Yisroel have each issued posters inviting all Jews in the Holy Land to meet the Rebbe. Posters have also been issued by the Toras Emes Yeshivah and Kolel Chabad.

Tuesday 29th Tammuz

The Rebbe arrived at 4 p.m. at Alexandria on his way to Eretz Yisroel. At the instigation of Senator Sir Joseph de Figato Bey the immigration authorities were instructed to facilitate the Rebbe's entry into Egypt and his continuing journey to Eretz Yisroel in every possible way. A government launch carried the Chief Rabbi's representative, Rabbi Daniel Gaon, to the ship before it docked to greet and welcome the Rebbe in the name of the Rabbinate and the Jewish community of Alexandria.

A group representing the Toras Emes Yeshivah and the Kolel Chabad came from Jerusalem to receive the Rebbe. The Rebbe stayed at the Hotel Regina Palace—Room 29. Food was sent to the Rebbe by his relation Rabbi Zvi Arye Schneersohn.

In the evening many representatives of the Jewish community, including Sir Joseph de Figato, called on the Rebbe. The Rebbe showed great interest in the situation of the Alexandrian Jews and requested that those present undertake to establish a yeshivah *in Alexandria. He was very pleased to hear from Rabbi Joseph Halevi that there was a* Beis Hamedrash *with set times for learning.*

Wednesday 1st Av

The Rebbe davenned shacharis in the Old Shul. He visited Sir Joseph de Figato and thanked him for the arrangements which he had made on his behalf. The Rebbe also visited the office of the Rabbinate where he was received with great honour. He next visited a number of shuls *and* Torah *establishments before being accompanied to the train by Sir Joseph de Figato, the Chief Rabbis and other senior communal representatives.*

The Rebbe arrived at Kantara where he was told by officials that the Government in Jerusalem had instructed them to facilitate the Rebbe's journey to Eretz Yisroel. *The Rebbe was accorded great honour and respect.*

Thursday 2nd Av

From early morning crowds from many towns and cities in Eretz Yisroel *flocked to the railway station at Lod. An official reception committee awaited the arrival of the Rebbe's train. Amongst them were the Chief Rabbis of Jerusalem and Tel Aviv, representatives of other towns and settlements,* menahelim *of* yeshivos, *the* menahel *and pupils of the Toras Emes Yeshivah, the Elders of* Anash *and representatives of Agudas Yisroel in the Holy Land and charitable institutions of Jerusalem.*

In the meantime a delegation of some thirty people welcomed the Rebbe at Rehovot and a similar number at B'er Yaacov, joining the train at these stops. The atmosphere was becoming more intense. At 6.40 a.m. the train arrived at Lod where the Rebbe was greeted with song and with great joy. There, the Rebbe changed to the Jerusalem train; a chain of hands being formed to shield him from the jostling and eager crowd. Eventually about 400 people joined the train to Jerusalem and during the journey many had the great zechus *to enter the Rebbe's compartment and see him privately.*

At the railway station in Jerusalem a similar scene was being enacted; crowds flocking on foot and by bus to catch a glimpse of the Rebbe. Here, too, representatives of the Chief Rabbis of Eretz Yisroel and a Guard of Honour awaited the Rebbe. By 9.15 a.m. when the train arrived at Jerusalem railway station a crowd of over 5,000 people had gathered. There appeared to be a sea of heads and one could hear people calling "Here is the Rebbe." The large crowd behaved with great dignity and respect.

On his arrival in Jerusalem the Rebbe rent his clothes and said the berocho: "Dayan Ho'Emes". The police Guard of Honour, headed by the Chief of Command Mr. Harrington and other Senior Officers, lined a path to the waiting room where the Rebbe was greeted by Rabbi Webber representing Rabbi Kook, the Chief Rabbi of Palestine; a representative of the Sephardi Chief Rabbi, the Rishon Le Zion, Rabbi Jacob Meir; a representative of Rabbi Yosef Chaim Sonnenfeld, the Av Beth Din of Jerusalem; the Gaon Rabbi Klotskin, the Lubliner Rav; Rabbi Charlap, the Rav of Shaare Chesed; Rabbi Vidal Surango; representatives of the Sephardi Community and the Secretary of the Sephardi Community, Mr. Cassatto. Also present was the venerable Chassid Rabbi Aronin, together with Rabbi Moshe Blau and Rabbi Reuven Shlomo Jungreis, the leaders of Agudas Yisroel in Eretz Yisroel; Rabbi Braunstein and Rabbi Rubin, the Principals of Chaye Olam; Rabbi Avrohom Aminoff, the Rav of the Bukharan Community; Rabbi Horowitz and Rabbi Chaim Leib Auerbach of the Yeshivas Shaare Hashomayim; Rabbi Nochum Yaffe representing the Kolel Volin; Rabbi Zalman Soloveitchik, Rabbi Nachman Gedalya Braude and Rabbi Hillel Rivlin representing the Vaad Haklolli; Rabbi, the Tzaddik, Avrohom Ber Twersky and his brother Rabbi Dovid Twersky, children of the Rebbe, Reb Nochamche, the Twersky Rebbe; Mr. Caspi, the Lithuanian Consul and many others.

The railway track itself and the forecourt of the station were crowded with people waiting to see the Rebbe. With great difficulty the police cleared a path to enable the Rebbe to reach his car which took him to the beautiful Hotel Amdorsky. Never before had Jerusalem witnessed such a reception. The newspapers, even the left-wing ones, printed articles welcoming the Rebbe. In the meantime a large crowd, eager to see the Rebbe and receive his blessing, had assembled outside the hotel and repeatedly called for him to appear on the balcony. The Rebbe acceded to their request and his appearance was greeted with singing. An elderly *person in the crowd loudly pronounced the* berocho: *"Blessed be The One who shared from His wisdom to those who fear Him."*

The Rebbe gave the crowd a berocho *which they received with great emotion.*

The Rebbe was visited in his hotel by Rabbi Sonnenfeld together with leaders of Agudas Yisroel in Eretz Yisroel, *Rabbi Yitzchok Frankel of the Beth Din of Jerusalem, Rabbi Shimon Horowitz,* Menahel of *Yeshivas Shaare Hashomayim, Rabbi Jacob Isaac Teitlebaum and the Elders of* Chabad. *At 4 p.m. the Rebbe left to* daven mincha *at the Kosel Ma'arovi. The news of this spread like wildfire and once again large numbers of people hurried to see the Rebbe. The route to the Kosel was so crowded that the Rebbe and his entourage reached it only with difficulty. One could now sense that something special was happening in our Holy City.*

Mincha *was recited with great emotion, just like* erev Yom Kippur. *Rabbi Yosef Shmodkin led the prayers. Following* mincha *a chair was brought for the Rebbe and he started to say* Tehillim. *The crowd was visibly moved by the prayers of the* Tzaddik *and his quiet crying as he prayed by the remains of our* Beis Hamikdosh. *Within minutes the crowd joined in the* Tehillim *being recited by the Rebbe with a pleasant tune and with great* dvekus *and their loud weeping could be clearly heard.*

When the Rebbe had finished his prayers he enquired of those near him whether it was the minhag *to kiss the Holy Stones. On receiving an affirmative reply the Rebbe's eyes filled with tears expressing a deep sadness at the Holy Wall. He inclined his head and the sound of him kissing the remains of our* Beis Hamikdosh *could be heard.*

With great difficulty a path was cleared for the Rebbe's return. On his way back from the Kosel, *the Rebbe visited the Gaon Rabbi Sonnenfeld. On hearing that the Rebbe was approaching, the elderly Gaon went out to greet him. They spent about half an hour together discussing* divrei Torah *and then parted with signs of great friendship.*

Friday 3rd Av

At 1 p.m. the Rebbe, accompanied by the menahel of the Toras Emes Yeshivah and some of the Elders of Chabad, visited the Chief Rabbi of Palestine, Rabbi Avrohom Yitzchok HaCohen Kook. Also present were Rabbi Charlap the Rav of Shaare Chesed and the Chief Rabbi's brother, Rabbi Dovber Kook the Rav of Afulla and many talmidei chachomim and Rabbis. The Rebbe was received very warmly by the Chief Rabbi who remarked to the Rebbe that although he had never met the Rebbe before it was, according to the Halacha, not incumbent upon him to recite the berocho "Shehecheyanu". However, his knowledge of the Rebbe through correspondence and his joy at now seeing him face to face gave him a strong desire to recite the berocho.

After discussing Torah and general matters concerning Jewry in Eretz Yisroel and the Diaspora they took leave of one another with great friendship.

Awaiting the Rebbe on the steps was Chief Rabbi Kook's mother. She asked the Rebbe for a berocho and the Rebbe responded with one for long life.

From there the Rebbe visited the Chief Rabbi of the Sephardi community, Rabbi Jacob Meir, who received him with obvious pleasure and great respect. As it was already late on Friday the visit was short and the Rebbe parted from Rabbi Meir with great love.

The Elders of Chabad and Anash came from all parts of Eretz Yisroel to spend Shabbos with the Rebbe. For Kabbolos Shabbos the large hall was crowded to capacity. The Rebbe prayed in a small hall near his room. After davenning the Rebbe entered the large hall to extend Shabbos greetings to those present.

Saturday 4th Av

In the morning the Rebbe had Maftir. He said the berocho "Hagomel" and then recited the Haphtorah with especial pleasantness. Towards the evening, crowds representative of all spheres of Jewish life in Eretz Yisroel started to gather at the hotel; Rabbis, great scholars, leaders of institutions, writers, *leading personalities, intellectuals,* Chassidim, *especially* Anash *and* Chabad Chassidim, *all jostling to obtain the best position to hear the* maamar *of* Chassidus *which the Rebbe was to deliver. In all, a few thousand people gathered on the roof of the hotel which had been specially lit for the occasion. At 6 p.m. the Rebbe, seated on a platform that had been erected before* Shabbos, *commenced the* maamar *which opened with the verse "Zion will be redeemed with Judgment and her captives with charity" (Isaiah 1:27). The* maamar *took two hours to recite and the Rebbe's holy words inflamed the hearts of those present.*

At 10 p.m. Chief Rabbi Kook accompanied by his son, Rabbi Zvi Yehuda Kook, returned the Rebbe's call of the previous day. The Rebbe received him with great honour and they stayed together a long time discussing Torah, Chassidus *and general matters.*

Sunday 5th Av

At 10 a.m. Rabbi Jacob Meir, accompanied by Rabbi Joseph Levi, one of the great Sephardi *Rabbis of Jerusalem and Lord Moshiach Borachev, the head of the* Sephardi *community, returned the Rebbe's visit.*

The Sephardi *Chief Rabbi apologised to the Rebbe for not having recited the* berocho *"Who shared from His wisdom . . . ." when the Rebbe visited him at his home. He commented on the difference between the text of the* berocho *which one recites when one meets a* talmid chochom *or,* lehavdil, *a wise non-Jew. In the first case the text read "shared His wisdom" whereas in the second case the text read "Who gave of His wisdom". This was because a* Tzaddik *was part of the* Al-ty. *Rabbi Meir expressed his happiness at having the* zechus *to meet the Rebbe. Later in the day the Rebbe visited his relative, Rabbi Nochamche Twersky.*

The Rebbe decided to visit the resting place of the Ari Z.L. (Rabbi Yitzchok Luria). He was accompanied by the menahel *of Toras Emes and others of* Anash. *At the main hotel in Afulla the Rebbe was visited by Rav Shlomo Aronson, the Chief Rabbi of Tel Aviv, who at that time had been staying on Mount Carmel for health reasons. They discussed matters of general interest and particularly the Rebbe's efforts on behalf of Jewry in Russia.*

At 5.30 p.m. the Rebbe arrived at Safed. Although the Rebbe's visit had been undertaken suddenly and the authorities there had been notified of his intended visit less than an hour earlier, a beautiful reception had been arranged at the hotel where the Rebbe was to stay. An assembly of all the Rabbis and leading citizens headed by Chief Rabbi Silberman awaited the Rebbe's arrival. Because he wished to visit the resting place of the Ari Z.L. *in daylight the Rebbe had only time to extend to them the greeting of "Shalom" before hurrying to* daven mincha. *Immediately following prayers, he travelled to the cemetery. In the meantime a large crowd had gathered at the resting place of the* Ari Z.L. *The Rebbe went to the tomb and first recited some prayers from the* siddur. *Then he raised his eyes to heaven, standing motionless, silent except for deep sobbing which seemed to melt the hearts of all those present so that they joined in the crying. The Rebbe read the* pidyonos *which he had brought with him and then walked around the tombs of the* Ari Z.L., *the* Ramak (*Rabbi Moshe Cordovero*) *and Rabbi Shlomo Alkabetz* (Lecho Dodi) *who are buried close to one another. The Rebbe then visited the tomb of Rabbi Joseph Caro who is buried nearby and continued alone to the resting place of Rabbi Moshe Alshech and spent some time there. Later in the evening the Rebbe walked up the mountain, a difficult task even for a younger man, especially after such a long tiring journey. The Rebbe walked with strong steps and a holy spirit; his strength surprised everyone present. Half-way up he rested on a chair which had been brought for him from town. He said to those present: "With the first visit to the Holy Places one becomes emotionally stirred to the extent that the physical world disappears." At the entrance to the cemetery the Sephardi Rabbis were waiting to greet the Rebbe. The Rebbe enquired of them whether they conducted public* shiurim *at their synagogues and was pleased with their affirmative reply. The Rebbe strengthened them with words of encouragement and gave them his holy blessing. The large crowd awaiting the Rebbe on his return to his hotel received him with great* simcha. *The Rebbe extended "Shalom" to everyone and gave them his blessing. He then went to rest for a while. Later, at his request, a small table was brought to him on the porch where he sat writing* Chassidus *for some three hours.*

Monday 6th Av

At 3 a.m. the Rebbe left to visit Meron, the resting place of the RaShBI leaving a specific sum of money for the needs of the Torah Institutions in Safed.

When the Rebbe (accompanied by many notables of Safed and Tiberias) arrived in Meron the sun had started to rise. He went to the cave of Rabbi Shimon ben Yochai and secluded himself there. He lit some candles and prayed at the grave, crying bitterly in a manner which stirred all who heard it. The Rebbe again read the pidyonos and gave instructions to daven speedily. Then he walked to the grave of Rabbi Eleazar ben Shimon where he recited some chapters of Psalms. The Rebbe circled the grave and went on his own to the cave of Rabbi Yitzchok Napacha. One of the Chassidim who entered the cave afterwards found a note written in the Rebbe's hand: "All the pupils who learn in Russia and Jewry in general are experiencing a deficiency in material and spiritual matters."

At the request of the gabbayim, the Rebbe went to visit the Yeshivas bar Yochai and the Old Age Home. The leaders of these Institutions received him with great honour and prepared a breakfast for all who accompanied the Rebbe. The Rebbe himself ate of the cake which he had brought with him. He signed his name in the Visitors' Book and wrote the date as "the 6th Av—may the Al-ty turn it to joy and happiness." At 9 a.m. the Rebbe arrived in Tiberias and went immediately to the tomb of Rabbi Meir Baal Haness. Here, too, he said a short prayer. In the meantime, the Rebbe's presence in the town had become known and people, young and old, rushed to greet him. They surrounded the Rebbe's car whilst he was on his way to visit the grave of Rabbi Mendel of Vitebsk. Through the window the Rebbe gave them "Shalom" and money with which to buy mashke, so that they should wish him success when saying "lechayim". The Jews of Tiberias received the Rebbe with great love and deep emotion. The Rebbe visited the tombs of Rabbi Mendel of Vitebsk, Rabbi Abraham Kalisk and others; he continued to the graves of Rabbi Akiva, Rabbi Yochanon ben Zakai, the Sheloh and the Rambam At the grave of the Rambam he stood in quiet contemplation for a while and as he left the grave the Rebbe said the verse from Koheles: "Vehachai yitain el liboh" ("and the one who is alive should take it to his heart"), explaining that a person should take it to heart that the life he lives should be an everlasting life—like Tzaddikim who even when they die are still referred to as being alive. He added that the merit to achieve this was possible only through the verse "Hayom Laasoisom" ("Today is the day to do it").

The Rebbe returned to his hotel where he gave "Shalom" and his blessings to the crowd which awaited him.
At 2 p.m. the Rebbe left for Jerusalem where he rested awhile before starting yechidus which continued until late into the night. He was visited also by Rabbi Tukchinsky and Rabbi Zalasnik, the Principals of the Yeshivah Etz Chaim.

Tuesday 7th Av

At 10 a.m. the Rebbe was visited by Dr. Wallach the Principal of the Shaare Zedek Hospital, Rabbi Shapiro of Drobych, a grandson of the Rhyzhiner Rebbe, and other leading personalities of Jerusalem. At 2 p.m. the Rebbe commenced his journey to Hebron. Several hundred people travelling in a cavalcade of cars accompanied him. Talmidim of the Yeshivas Toras Emes, Chassidim and the elders of Anash joined the Rebbe for his journey.
At Beth Lechem the Rebbe visited the Tomb of Rachel and he questioned in which direction the body had been interred so as to pray facing the head. The Rebbe's countenance portrayed the elation of his soul as he prayed and wept. He circled the tomb and again read the pidyonos. He lit eighteen candles before leaving the tomb.
The cars then moved on towards Hebron. When they reached the Settlement of Migdal Aiden, a group of people led by the Askenazi and Sephardi Rabbis of the town came to welcome him. He extended the greeting of "Shalom" and blessed them. On reaching Hebron, the Rebbe stopped for a while at the home of his relative, Rabbi Yaacov Yosef Slonim, and from there went on to visit the cave of Machpelah. The Rebbe prayed mincha with the Dvekus Nigun of Rosh Hashonoh which moved everyone present to tears. He circled the area and then went inside.[1]

After leaving Machpelah the Rebbe went to inspect his inheritance in Hebron.[2]

He interested himself in all the details of the area, the condition of the buildings and the plots around it. He again visited the home of Rabbi

[1] An account of the Rebbe's visit here is given in a separate article on page 32.
[2] The Rebbe had inherited properties in Hebron from his father Rabbi Sholom Dovber.

Slonim where he rested awhile before going to the large shul *which was crowded to capacity. The Rebbe said a* maamar *of Chassidus based on the verse "May our G–d be with us." (1 Kings 8:57.)*

He visited the Slobodka Yeshivah in Hebron at the special request of its leaders and returned to Jerusalem at 10 p.m.

Before his journey to Hebron, the Rebbe visited the Kolel Chabad and showed great interest in all its activities. He expressed great joy at seeing an Institution which was founded by his forbears, the Holy Rebbes of Chabad.

Wednesday 8th Av

The Rebbe set aside erev *Tisha B'Av for* yechidus *for the* talmidim *of the Yeshivas Toras Emes.*

Thursday 9th Av

On Tisha B'Av *the Rebbe went to the Mount of Olives to visit the resting places of Zechariah Hanovi, Rabbi Chaim ben Attar (the author of Or HaChayim), the tomb of Shimon Hatzaddik, the tombs of the Sanhedrin Ketana and of the Sanhedrin Gedoloh, the courtyard of Kalba Savuoh and the burial places of the Kings of David. He showed interest in the order of the graves and the burial chambers. When one of his entourage said that these resting places were very dear ones the Rebbe replied that it will be interesting when all those resting here are raised up to life.* Motzei *Tisha B'Av was set aside especially for the Yeshiva Toras Emes. The* hanholah *of the* yeshivah *arranged a large meal there following the Fast and the Rebbe ate together with the* menahelim, talmidim *and some elders of* Anash.

When the Rebbe entered the yeshivah *it was as if his face was lit by an inner joy. Those present said "lechayim" and sang Chassidic* nigunim *in which the Rebbe joined. The Rebbe then delivered a discourse, a free translation of which is as follows:*

"I asked to farbreng *with the* talmidim. *As a general introduction to this evening, I would mention that the Toras Emes Yeshivah was founded in 1912 when pupils were sent here from Tomchei Tmimim to be as seeds and plants. It should be known that the purpose of the*

stablishment was to radiate light. Thank G–d, the Yeshivas Toras
Emes has already produced mashgichim and mashpi'im. However, I
still feel it necessary on my first visit here to explain specifically the
purpose which prompted the establishment of Tomchei Tmimim.[1]
So I will repeat here the actual words spoken at that time by my father
on Sunday 15th Elul 5657 (1897). It was at the time of my wedding
that my father called in a few Chassidic baalei battim to discuss the
establishment of a Lubavitch yeshivah. He said that it was not just for
the sake of Torah learning. 'Thank G–d,' he said, 'there are many yeshivos
and generally in this district Torah is not lacking. The purpose of founding
another yeshivah is to radiate light. The students should learn Nigleh and
they should learn Chassidus and the interaction of the two should equip
them to fulfil that purpose.'
It is not my intention to detract from the image of other yeshivos but
rather to emphasise that the purpose of this yeshivah is to shed spiritual
light. On another occasion my father said that the inner meaning of the
blessings which we recite on the Torah is as we say in the text '. . . Nosan
lonoo Toras Emes vechayai olom nota besoichainoo'—'Who has
given us a Law of Truth and has planted everlasting life in our midst.'
Torah should illuminate the world and elevate the world to G–dliness.
Now that over thirty years have elapsed since Tomchei Tmimim was
established, one can assess the tmimim[2] and observe their strength and
mesiras nefesh for Torah. When one considers the pressures on them and
the difficulties which they experience inside the Beis Hamedrash and
generally in Russia, their situation breaks one's heart. But all this is when
one stands on the ground. If, however, one lifts oneself a hand's-breadth higher
one can see that in relation to the purpose of the soul descending into the body, the
handing down of the Torah and the creation of the world generally, their great
mesiras nefesh is a wonderful thing. Their suffering is hard to endure—
'reducing fat and blood'—not enough food—not enough sleep. But again this is
when viewed from the ground. When one raises oneself a hand's-breadth higher
their mesiras nefesh is a very great thing. One can already observe pupils of
pupils; children of ten to twelve years of age go happily to prison for the
sake of learning, refusing, often under pain of torture, to divulge the names of
their teachers.
Toras Emes is a continuation of and a branch of Tomchei Tmimim.
The first pupils were products of Tomchei Tmimim and more and more
have been added—kain yirboo. One must hope that this strength of mesiras
nefesh will not continue to be necessary; that the Al–ty will remove
the pressures so that there will no longer be any obstacles to observing Torah

[1] See CHALLENGE an encounter with Lubavitch–Chabad, page 49 et seq.

[2] Students of Tomchei Tmimim yeshivos are called tmimim.

and Mitzvos. *These obstacles affect everyone, not only those in Russia but everywhere in the world, for the entire globe is in exile. They are tests and obstacles that one has to overcome.*

"*Generally one's life in this world—120 years—is transient, but one must use it to illuminate the world and to elevate the world to Torah. My father appointed me General Menahel of all the* yeshivos. *By his life in this world and by his life in the higher world, he instructs and warns me that I can only lead* yeshivos *which pursue this objective of illuminating the world with Torah. And as the encompassing light and the light of the zechus of our Nassi shines on and surrounds Toras Emes this should give you the strength to radiate light in the world.*

"*Really we should* farbreng *in detail but I am sure that the* mashpiah *and* menahel *farbreng with you often and that you are well aware of basic fundamental matters. Also, we are limited for time. One has to say* Chassidus *too and this should be noted by you and by me, even though the* mashpiah *has told me that you learn* Chassidus *and that there are also such among you who are capable of the* avodah *of* tefillah; tefillah *being not just the opposite of 'not praying' but* avodah shebalev,—*Divine Service of the heart—which is* davenning. *Nevertheless I must reiterate that our purpose is to bring light into the world—so that the world should not lower the person but that the person should elevate the world to Torah.*"

After the sichah, *the Rebbe delivered a* maamar *of Chassidus "Ato horaiso lodaas"—"To you it was shown that you might know. . . ." (Deuteronomy 4:35.)*

Before he left the hall, the Rebbe invited all the talmidim *of the yeshivah to gather around him and he took his leave of them with the following blessing:*

"*May you all be well. I am travelling away but we are not really parting. Place is not important so we are not really separating. Each one of you should be as ten thousand to radiate light. May the Al-ty grant that the power of our Nassi who gives us the strength in our G-dly service, in learning and* avodah shebalev, *should help you. May it be as the expression in the verse 'Veyidgoo lorov bekerev haaretz'—'They should multiply in the Land.' (Genesis 48:16.) It should be* v'Torah-or—*and Torah is light. Be well and good night.*"

Friday 10th Av

10 a.m. *The Rebbe visited the Diskin Orphanage, where he was received by the Gaon Rabbi Yosef Chaim Sonnenfeld, Rabbi Klotskin and the other members of the Administrative Committee. He continued on to the Old Age Home, the hospital of Dr. Wallach and the Bikur Cholim Hospital.*
1 p.m. *The Rebbe was visited by his relative Rabbi Nochamche Twersky and his sons.*

Shabbos 11th Av

A special rostrum had been erected in the big tent which had been converted into a hall to accommodate the large crowd which had gathered to listen to the Rebbe deliver a Maamar of Chassidus. The great joy experienced by the listeners was expressed by everyone saying: "We wish the Rebbe Shlito would remain in Jerusalem for another few Shabbosos and that we should have the merit to listen to many more discourses like this."

Sunday 12th Av

The Rebbe devoted the whole day to visiting his relatives and the following Institutions:
The Yeshivas Medrash Shloime where he met the Elders and leaders of the Bukharan community. The Talmud Torah of Bukharan Jews which is under the auspices of Agudas Yisroel. He was received by the Principals, Rabbi Moshe Blau and Rabbi Moshe Porush. The pupils of the Talmud Torah welcomed the Rebbe by singing "Boruch Habo". The Talmud Torah Doresh Zion.
From there the Rebbe went to say farewell to the Gaon Rabbi Jacob Meir, the Sephardi Chief Rabbi, spending about half an hour with him in his house. Afterwards the Rebbe visited the Yeshivas Ohel Yaacov which was under the leadership of Rabbi Jacob Meir and also the Boruchov Orphanage, where the Rebbe signed the Visitors' Book.
Together with Rabbi Jacob Meir, the Rebbe called upon the Gaon Rabbi Yosef Chaim Sonnenfeld. They visited the Misgov Ladoch Hospital, the Yeshivas Porat Yosef, the Yeshivas Shaare Hashomayim, the shul called the Churba of Reb Yehuda haChassid, the Yeshivah and Talmud Torah Etz Chaim and the Yeshivas Mea Shearim. In Mea Shearim,

apart from the residents of the area, a crowd of several thousand people thronged the streets. The Rebbe blessed the assembled crowd before visiting the Chabad Shul, Beis Menachem (now called Tzemach Tzedek) in the Old City. From there he went to pay a farewell visit to Chief Rabbi Koo with whom he spent about an hour discussing various matters. Afterwards he paid another visit to Rabbi Nochamche Twersky.

Monday 13th Av

7 a.m. The Rebbe paid his second visit to the Kosel. As he approached The Wall his eyes, full of love, dvekus and spiritual elevation, took in the whole area. He expressed his excitement and poured out his heart in prayers and tears. The Rebbe was particularly interested in the building projects near the Kosel. On his way back, the Rebbe explained the expression of our Sages "No man ever said to his fellow: 'I have not room to lodge overnight in Jerusalem.'" (Avos 5:5.) Our Sages used the Hebrew term "mokom"—"place"—and not the term "zeman"—"time"—for in "place" no matter how overcrowded one can always squeeze oneself in but as far as "time" is concerned there is never enough. The Rebbe added: "During the 12 days that I have been in Jerusalem I have gained a lot, Boruch Hashem, and I have achieved a lot. I visited every place. By 'every place' I mean many places which, as a beginning, is enough. I leave Jerusalem taking with me the tremendous impression it has made on me. May the Al–ty grant that Moshiach should be revealed soon so that the passing of time should not cool the feelings I have." Later the Rebbe was visited by the Chief Justice of the High Court, Mr. Gad Frumkin.

From early morning a large crowd started to assemble near the Rebbe's hotel, waiting to receive the Rebbe's blessing as he left the Holy City. 10 a.m. The Rebbe left his hotel and entered a waiting car. Through the window of the car he gave his parting blessing to all those present. The Rebbe was escorted by the Principals and pupils of Yeshivas Toras Emes, the Elders of Chabad and Anash. Rabbi Nochamche Twersky and his sons followed in another car escorting the Rebbe to the Settlement at Moza where they said their farewells. En route to Tel Aviv, near Mikvei Yisroel, the Rebbe was met by a special delegation from the Chief Rabbi of Tel Aviv and leading personalities of the city and the Elders of Anash.

11 a.m. *The Rebbe arrived in Tel Aviv. The few hundred people who accompanied him entered the town with great joy singing* Chabad *melodies. Large crowds thronged all the streets through which the Rebbe's car passed. At the Hotel Sfas Hayam the large crowd which had gathered greeted the Rebbe with joy. He returned their greetings and gave them his blessing. Following his arrival the Rebbe was visited by Rabbi Eliyahu Aaron Milikovsky, the Rav of Kharkov. Later the Rebbe gave* yechidus *to* Anash *and leading personalities of the town. The* yechidus *went on until a late hour in the evening.*

Tuesday 14th Av

10 a.m. *The Rebbe was visited by Rabbi Avraham Abichzir, the Rav of Alexandria.*

11 a.m. *The Rebbe was visited by his relation, Rabbi Shneur Slonim, the* Chassidic *Rav of Tel Aviv-Jaffa, who spent a long time with him. The Rebbe was visited too by the leading citizens of the Municipality of Tel Aviv whom he received cordially . He said that when he was in Russia he thought that there were no longer "party" differences between Jews because when the head receives a hard knock it is not only the head that suffers—the whole body is affected. Since leaving Russia he had unfortunately seen, to his great distress, that Jews were still divided by "parties"—then he reminded himself of his own "party" whose aim is "strengthening the observance of* Torah *and* mitzvos".

Later, representatives of many Settlements visited the Rebbe inviting him to visit them. Because of the shortage of time the Rebbe was only able to accept the invitations from Petach Tikvah and Bnei Brak.

At Petach Tikvah notices were posted announcing the Rebbe's visit and a special reception was arranged. A delegation was sent to Tel Aviv to escort the Rebbe. At 4 p.m. the Rebbe, accompanied also by the Principals and pupils of Yeshivas Toras Emes and the Elders of Anash, *travelled to Petach Tikvah. An official public reception had been arranged near the Settlement* shul. *The large assembly which had gathered there headed by all the communal leaders greeted the Rebbe with great joy. He expressed great interest in the spiritual situation of the Settlement, and discussed many matters with them, especially in relation to education and the fixing of times for learning. The Rebbe gave them all his blessing. The Rebbe then visited the Yeshivas Lomze in Petach Tikvah. At the* yeshivah *he was received by the Principal and* Roshei Yeshivah *with the greeting of "Boruch Habo".*

Inside the yeshivah, which was full to capacity, the Rebbe was warmly welcomed in a speech by its Principal who commented on the great zechus the yeshivah had to welcome such a guest. The Rebbe replied with a blessing: "Uvo Letzion . . ." and the wish that the Torah light should shine on them and permeate them with a spirit of knowledge and Yiras Hashem.

A gevir who had donated the large building asked the Rebbe for a blessing that he should be able to repay the money which he had borrowed for the project. The Rebbe expressed the hope that the Al–ty should help him to spend ten times as much for such holy purposes and he gave him a berocho for parnossa and that he should have the zechus that the light of Torah should shine on him.

On his way to Tel Aviv the Rebbe stopped at Bnei Brak. Here, too, an official reception had been arranged in the shul. Tables had been set with choice wines, confectionery and cakes, and candles were lit in honour of the guest. The Rebbe expressed interest in their spiritual and financial situation, especially in chinuch and times for learning Torah. He wished them good parnossa, that they should set times for learning Torah and that they should raise their children in Torah and mitzvos.

6 p.m. The Rebbe returned to Tel Aviv. He received Anash for yechidus. The Gaon Rabbi Shaul, Rav of Viroshov visited him.

Thursday 16th Av

10 a.m. The Rebbe left Tel Aviv for the railway station at Lod. He was seen off by the Principals and pupils of Yeshivas Toras Emes, leading personalities of Tel Aviv, Elders of Anash and Chabad from Tel Aviv, Jaffa, Jerusalem and other Holy Cities.

At the time of departing the Rebbe was very emotional. He expressed his blessing to everyone and with a special show of love he parted from the pupils of the yeshivah.

Owing to pressure of time he was unable to deliver the maamar of Chassidus which he had intended. So he left the maamar in his own handwriting with them. He then left by train for Egypt on his way to the U.S.A.

During the Rebbe's stay in Eretz Yisroel everyone close to Yiddishkeit was imbued with a high holy spirit. The light and warmth which he radiated, the impression which his visit had engraved on each heart, would never be erased.

Rabbi Joseph Isaac Schneersohn, the late Lubavitcher Rebbe, arriving in the U.S.A., following his visit to *Eretz Yisroel* in 1929.

1948

Ooforatzto

"...and you shall spread out..."

Genesis 28 : 14

From the beginnings pioneered by the small band of dedicated and selfless *Chassidic* settlers almost 200 years ago, *Chabad* institutions and influence in *Eretz Yisroel* grew apace. Each generation produced the right leaders for the communities which had been established in Hebron, Jerusalem and in other smaller centres. Great in learning and wisdom, guided by the Lubavitcher Rebbe of their time, they overcame the hardships and immense difficulties with which life in *Eretz Yisroel* abounded. Augmented by later *Chassidic* immigrants they tenaciously built the institutions which were to become the foundations on which the present *Chabad* ramifications in Israel were established and expanded.

From 1948, first under the direction of the late Lubavitcher Rebbe, Rabbi Joseph Isaac Schneersohn, and then of his successor, Rabbi Menachem Mendel Schneerson שליט״א, the work of *Chabad* in Israel gained impetus.

The new and exciting challenges of a changing and evolving society required new approaches and answers. *Chabad*'s ability to meet these challenges within the fundamental framework and without compromise, its ability to successfully address the young, the hostile, the estranged and the indifferent and its ability to demonstrate the relevance of *Torah* in a modern society has won the respect and admiration of all.

The *Chabad* villages, first Kfar Chabad and, more recently, Nachalat Har Chabad were established. *Yeshivos*, day schools, vocational schools and seminaries were set up and expanded. *Barmitzvah* classes, evening classes and *shiurim* sprang up. Annual and day camps became a feature of *Chabad*'s work. Conferences for youth from Israel and abroad at which ideas and views might be interchanged, absorption of immigrants, community centres, apartment blocks—all these, and more, were undertaken by *Chabad*. Campaigns for the observance of *mitzvos* such as *Tefillin* and *lulav* and *esrog* spread throughout the land and it was soon found that it was difficult to resist the importuning of the often youthful, always cheerful *Chabadnik* who asked: "Have you put on *Tefillin* yet today?" or "Perhaps you left home too early to *bentsch lulav* and *esrog*?"

Visits to army camps and posts, *kibbutzim* and out-of-the-way settlements to spread the message of *Chassidus*; and if the welcome the first time was less rapturous than might be hoped for, the second time was invariably better and subsequent visits were usually as a result of cordial invitations.

Book and art exhibitions, music festivals, all became a regular part of the *Chabad* programme; a programme designed to bring every Jew in Israel nearer to his Source.

Chabad with its distinct philosophy and its programme of education at all levels and for all ages has proved to be the only religious catalyst to which the secular groups in modern Israel have reacted favourably and with enthusiasm.

"*Chabadniks*" soon became a term of endearment in the modern Hebrew language; a synonym for friendship, patience and concern.

It is not possible within this book to mention every school, each *yeshivah*. Neither, unfortunately, is it possible to portray every aspect of *Chabad*'s efforts. (Who else but *Chabad* could mount a campaign at *Purim* to deliver 18,000 *shalach monos* to soldiers, using planes, trucks, helicopters and jeeps and not have a single photograph of the event!)

It is hoped, however, that what follows will whet the reader's appetite to discover more for himself, so that on his next visit to Israel he will seek out *Chabad*.

Where will he find *Chabad*? Not just in those places which are distinctively *Chabad*. *Chabadniks* will also be found in the fields, in the factories, in *kibbutzim*, in towns and villages, in the forces; doing a worthwhile job, participating in the building up of the Holy Land.

How will he be recognised? It is not difficult. For whether at work or at a *farbrengen*, whether addressing an audience of hundreds in an auditorium, or a group in a *kibbutz* or at Suez, or just speaking one-to-one to a fellow-Jew, he will be bringing a message of faith and hope in friendship and with love.

Some of the *mitzvah* campaigns at the festivals of *Chanukah* and *Succos*.

at the Canal . . .

Chabadniks visit soldiers serving at the Suez Canal, bringing the Word of the Guardian of Israel to the guardians of Israel.

delivering *Shalach monos* . . . by air

Purim . . .

. . . by vehicle

. . . and on foot.

in the Forces...

at Music Festivals . . .

These festivals bring to large audiences the warmth and belief of *Chabad* in music and words. Recordings of these wonderful occasions are in great demand throughout the world.

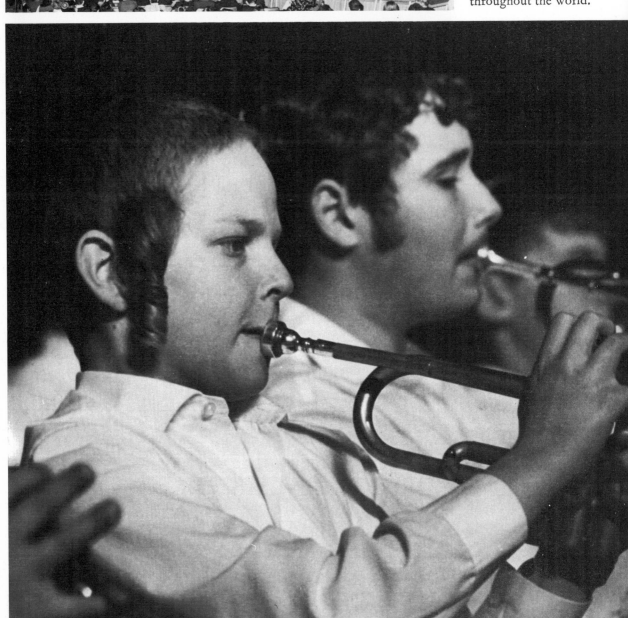

Jacques Lipchitz, world-
famous sculptor, and Baruch
Nachshon, both *Chabadniks*,
at the opening of the Jacques
Lipchitz Exhibition at the
Israel Museum, Jerusalem.

. . . and Exhibitions

Above: Kapporos. Bronze sculpture by Jacques Lipchitz. Ingersol Collection, Philadelphia.

Top: Kapporos ceremony at Kfar Chabad.

Above: President Shazar at a *Chabad* Book Exhibition.

Below: A Biblical Exhibition.

Above: David Ben Gurion, Israel's first Prime Minister, visits *Chabad* Exhibition.

Below: President Shazar at a Biblical Exhibition.

at Work . . .

at Farbrengens . . .

Farbrengens and special occasions at Kfar Chabad and other centres attract crowds and visitors from all over the world.

at Kiryat Arba

Above left: New Settlement at Kiryat Arba.

Far left: Children at play behind barbed wire at Kiryat Arba.

Near left: A *shiur* at the new *yeshivah*.

Top: Baruch Nachshon, noted Israeli artist, with his wife on the steps of Machpelah, following the circumcision of their seventh child there. A former student at the Lubavitch Yeshivah, Baruch Nachshon, following his military service, was encouraged by the Lubavitcher Rebbe שליט״א to develop his artistic talents by studying in New York. Returning to Israel, he settled after the Six-Day War at the new *Chabad* Settlement at Kiryat Arba. A recent one-man show of his work at the Jewish Museum, Berkeley, California, was most enthusiastically received. Many of his works are inspired by verses from the Psalms.

Above: An art lesson for an elder son.

Below left: Yehudi Menuhin. *Below right:* Arye Eliav.

Famous personalities visiting Kfar Chabad are invited to put on *Tefillin*.

Below: Rabbi E. Wolff, Executive Director of Chabad Vocational Schools, with Mr. Arye Pincus, Chairman of the Jewish Agency.

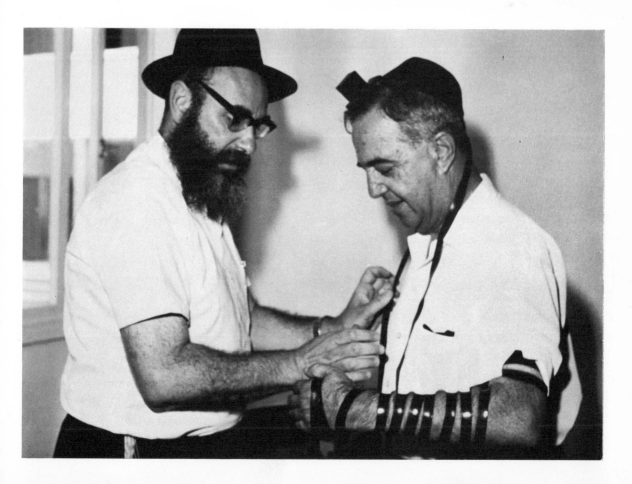

Chabad teaching and literature abound with references to the unlimited potential for good in each individual. This potential could hardly be better demonstrated than by the late Rabbi Yonah Eidelkop. Even amongst the many activist workers for spreading *Yiddishkeit* in Israel he was unique.

It was through his untiring efforts in founding educational establishments throughout the land that some 10,000 boys and girls receive religious instruction today in the Chadorim Torah Or. Here they are

imbued with the true values of Judaism.

At first his efforts to obtain support from communal leaders were often met with opposition and sometimes ridicule, but he eventually achieved great success, impressing everyone with his sincerity and personal self-sacrifice.

Rabbi Yonah Eidelkop had no official title in the *Chabad* organisation but was known throughout Israel by everyone as Rabbi Yonah *Oiseh Yiddishkeit*—Yonah "the maker of *Yiddishkeit*".

Publications in many languages and on a wide variety of subjects are printed and distributed by *Chabad*. The subject-matter ranges from philosophical discourses to children's books. With the influx of immigrants from Russia, texts and booklets in Russian were immediately available. A monthly magazine, *In the Vineyards of Chabad*, is produced as is a regular *Chabad* Bulletin. Both publications have a wide circulation.

ב"ה

Н. ИЗАКСОН

ХАНУКА

Исторический обзор,
описание, рассказы

Перевод с английского
— Н. С. Г. —

MERKOS L'INYONEI

5729

תש"כט

...одеться в праздничное ...наступающего шаббата. Таким образом он смог быть у Ханукальных огней в то время, когда их зажигали. Он видел, как отец зажигает Ханукальные лампадки, а затем, как мать зажигает Свечи шаббата. Теперь Иаков придвинул стул и сел вблизи Ханукального светильника.

Конечно же, он услышал знакомый голос Первой лампадки. «Добрый тебе вечер шаббата и хануки! Рад видеть тебя. Это младшая моя сестричка. Поздоровайся, сестричка, с этим маленьким моим другом!».

«Здравствуй, сказала Вторая Ханукальная лампадка, сделав грациозный реверанс. Я также знаю чудесный рассказ. Хочешь ты его послушать?».

«Конечно, хочу, ответил маленький Иаков. Прошу тебя, расскажи мне».

«Хорошо, сказала лампадка, слушай же».

И лампадка начала: «Иуда Маккабей повел маленький отряд правоверных евреев от победы к победе. Знаешь ли ты, что такое «партизанская война»? Это война, которую ведут малочисленные отряды против значительно превосходящих сил противника. Это и делали Иуда и его товарищи. Прячась в пещерах и устраивая засады, они внезапно нападали на врага с тыла или приближались к нему под покровом ночи. Несмотря на свою малочисленность, им удавалось каждый раз наносить противнику все новые поражения.

15

Антиоха обуяла ярость. Он посылал одну армию за другой, чтобы изловить Иуду и уничтожить его отряды, но его генералы все время терпели поражения. Наконец Антиох послал своего лучшего полководца Лизиаша с огромной армией, состоявшей из пехоты, кавалерии и боевых колесниц.

«... Они пришли с колесницами..., а мы именем Б-га!»

Иуда обратился к горсточке своих мужественных соратников: «Сегодня мы подвергнемся величайшему испытанию, сказал он. Но не бойтесь. Не наше оружие наносило поражения врагу до этого, побеждала наша вера в Б-га. Враг пришел к нам с колесницами и полагается на свою мощь. Мы же воюем именем Б-га, и Он будет за нас».

Призывая имя Б-га и оглашая воздух звуком труб, Иуда и его храбрые боевые друзья бросились на своих врагов. Увидев во главе отряда

Reactions

FROM LETTERS RECEIVED . . .

"The words of your speaker were deeply moving. In actual fact, he removed from us the 'fear' which the non-religious members had of religious people. They followed him in his singing, which presented to them an experience of authentic songs which came from the heart and entered the heart.

The whole of the evening showed to our members that there is a greatness and depth to Judaism. There were definitely many who began to think in their hearts about the distance between us and true Judaism.

Throughout the evening we felt the spark of Jewish brotherly love."

"Dear Friends,

It is very pleasant for me to thank you for the fine evening of enlightenment which you presented on your visit to our kibbutz. The power of faith within you is a never ending fountain of action, deeds and training for love of one's fellow-Jew. Although in other ways this is still not understandable to us, this must be respected and appreciated.

I do not exaggerate the reaction of the whole audience, adult and young, who testify to the fact that you know how to 'capture' us and implant within us your outlook and teach us to understand you.

May you be blessed."

From letters received . . . contd.

"Dear Friends,
I wish to express to you the deep gratitude of all who
were present at the Chabad *evening which took place*
this week. We had the privilege of coming into contact
with the profundity of your way of life and to yearn
for its spirit. Many will remember that evening and
will treasure it in their hearts as a rare experience.
Accept our blessings and best wishes and our hope
that you will continue to succeed in your way."

"I would like to thank you on behalf of the Directors of
our school for the interesting evening which you arranged
for us and for the beautiful way it was presented, for
the profound talk by your speaker and for the sweet and
moving Chabadnik *spirit he conveyed. The visit was*
tastefully arranged on a splendid scale. The applause
of the audience demonstrated your great influence and
the effect you had on us. It was a moving experience
which made us feel as one family."

FROM THE PRESS

"Chabad *in particular seems to have discovered an approach which the non-religious finds sympathetic and as a result its members are universally respected.*"

"*The Mayor of the city of Lod recently visited the Lubavitcher Rebbe* שליט"א *and presented the Rebbe with a golden key to the city.*

The key was presented as a token of appreciation of his activities in the development of the city, both in the spiritual and material sense. There are a substantial number of Chabad *educational institutions in Lod and recently a* Chabad *residential project was erected there.*

A few years ago the key to the city of Kiryat Gat was presented to the Lubavitcher Rebbe as a token of appreciation of Chabad *services to that city.*"

"Chabad *settlements in Israel are universally respected for their hard work and harmonious relationships, but the one quality above all others which has earned the* Chabad Chassidim *the respect and affection of all Jews is their genuine and unconditional love for all their fellow-Jews. Though scrupulously orthodox and theo-centric, the Lubavitchers never slight other Jews whose views differ from theirs, or question their Jewishness; they are devoid of any bitterness or a 'holier-than-thou' attitude and they attempt to win over other Jews by reason and example. In this way they make their own inestimable contribution to the warp and weft of Jewish life.*"

Right: The Mayor
of Lod visits
yeshivah.

Opposite top: Happy
youngsters enjoy a
break from learning.

Opposite bottom:
Chabad school and a
housing project
at Lod.

Opposite top: A *shiur* at Lod
Yeshivah.

Opposite bottom: Two new
immigrants from Russia (fore-
ground) receive instruction at Lod
Yeshivah.

Above: Cheder in Lod.

"...thou shalt meditate
therein day and night..."

(Joshua 1:8)

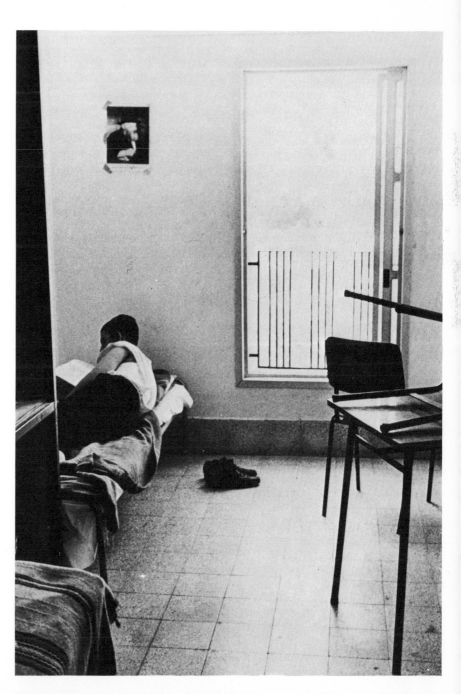

The Lubavitcher Rebbe שליט״א has stressed time and time again the need to renew the ancient custom of providing, to as wide a circle as possible, *matzos* baked according to the most stringent requirements (hand-baked *shemura matzos*).

For some years now the Chabad Youth Organisation—Zeirei Agudas Chabad—has, as one of its many activities, been baking such *matzos* for distribution to community leaders and to the general public.

The Chabad Youth Organisation—the criterion of "youth" in this context being spirit, not age—concerns itself with the spiritual needs of Jews and strives ceaselessly to familiarise them with the basic concepts and practices of Judaism. It is this *Chabad* organisation which arranges all the "action" campaigns, such as *Tefillin*, *lulav* and *esrog*, and *shalach monos*.

Some of the thousands of children who visit Kfar Chabad annually to watch baking of *shemura matzos*.

Inception of Barmitzvah Institute by Chabad Youth Movement

Within the framework of the activities of the Chabad Youth Movement in spreading *Yiddishkeit* amongst youth, an institute for preparing young boys for *Barmitzvah* has been opened for those who have an insufficient acquaintance with Jewish observances and customs. Its purpose is to create an awareness of Jewish values and practice and inculcate in the students of the institute an ability to realise them when they become of age.

The students receive an intensive course in basic Judaism over a period of several months.

One of the wings of the Chabad Youth House in Kfar Chabad is devoted to this institute.

Letter giving details of Barmitzvah Institute.

Yigal Yadin's biggest discovery
— in his heart

This article is reprinted from the Israeli publication *Integration*.

Throughout Israel this story is being told. It concerns a priceless religious discovery and Professor Yigal Yadin, Israel's leading archaeologist and former Chief of Staff of Israel's Army. Recently, Professor Yadin discovered a pair of *Tefillin* of the time of the Second Temple, some 2,000 years old, and had just given a lecture in Tel Aviv on his discovery. At the end of his talk, Professor Yadin described an experience he had had on his train journey from Jerusalem to Tel Aviv.

His train had stopped at Kfar Chabad, where a number of *Lubavitcher Chassidim* came on board. One of the *Chassidim*, as is the *Lubavitcher* wont, began asking passengers to don *Tefillin* and to recite the usual prayer.

"PERSEVERED"

"When he approached me," said Professor Yadin, "I told him that I did not wish to be bothered, that I was not religious and did not believe in the practice. The *Chassid* persevered and I asked him where he came from. He replied that he had managed to get out of Russia only two years ago.

"I asked him: 'Did you put on *Tefillin* in Russia?' He looked hard at me and replied that he had put on *Tefillin* every day since his *Barmitzvah*. I said to myself: 'Here is a man (he was about thirty-eight) who was born and raised under Communist rule, and who has yet never missed putting on *Tefillin*. How can I refuse him?'

"I was ashamed. Under Russian oppression, Jews put on *Tefillin* and here in the Jewish State, where we have freedom, Yigal Yadin refuses. I put on the *Tefillin*, recited the *Shema* and thanked him for giving me the opportunity. The *Chassid*'s face shone.

"After I had taken off the *Tefillin*, an elderly woman came over and said: 'The *Lubavitcher* didn't recognise you, but I know who you are. You are General Yadin, the archaeologist. Seeing you put on *Tefillin* has given me great pleasure.' And she told me her story."

"LAST WISH"

"'My son was also a *Chassid* of *Lubavitch*. He was the only religiously observant parachutist in his unit. He put on *Tefillin* every day. During the Six-Day War, my son was mortally wounded. As he lay on the desert sand in critical condition, his comrades asked him what was his last wish. "Put on *Tefillin*," my son barely answered and died. There and then, in turn, all his fellow-parachutists, officers and men, put on my son's *Tefillin*.'

"The old lady then showed me a picture of her son and I remembered that I, too, was carrying photographs of the ancient *Tefillin* I had found and which had never been displayed in public. I was overwhelmed by this chance meeting with the *Lubavitcher* and the bereaved mother on the train. It was unbelievable and very moving. I felt that I would break down. I took out my pictures and showed them to the mother. So she was the first to see my discovery. The elderly woman looked at the pictures and we both began to cry."

Train journey from Jerusalem to Tel Aviv. *Chabadniks* encourage passengers to don *Tefillin*.

Camp Gan Israel

The purpose of these camps, named after Rabbi Israel Baal Shem Tov the founder of the *Chassidic* movement, is to enable school children to spend their holidays in an authentic *Chassidic* atmosphere.

A camp for boys and one for girls, each extending over a twelve-day period, is held every year. A full programme of prayer, *Torah* classes, physical recreation, sports, swimming and social activities is arranged.

The hundreds of boys and girls who attend the camps each year leave refreshed spiritually and physically after an enjoyable, worthwhile, if hectic, holiday.

For those who are not able to attend the annual camps, special day camps are held each year. Boys and girls are taken on outings and visits, and at the same time are taught observances.

Jerusalem

In 1961, in an almost desolate section in the north-west of Jerusalem, on an area having a magnificent view of the Judean mountains and the ancient historical sites of Nov, the city of *Kohanim*, Givat Shaul, the Tomb of Samuel and the Tombs of the Sanhedrin, there commenced work on Shikun Chabad, which today is the headquarters of *Chabad* activities in Jerusalem.

Left and below: Shikun Chabad, Jerusalem—apartment buildings.

Opposite top: Pupils at Shikun Chabad Talmud Torah.

Opposite bottom left: Class at Talmud Torah.

Opposite bottom right: Talmud Torah School bus brings pupils from outside the district.

The complex now consists of apartment blocks providing accommodation at reasonable rentals, a synagogue and a large Communal Centre especially designed to accommodate young people and their activities. In 1962, the Shikun Chabad Talmud Torah was established to provide a *Chassidic* education not only for the *Chabad Chassidic* families in Jerusalem but also for many others who are intent on availing themselves of the high standard of education which is provided. The *Talmud Torah* has grown considerably and transport is available to bring children from other parts of Jerusalem. The school restaurant provides meals for the students.

There soon followed a kindergarten, "Gan Chanah", catering for girls between three and six years of age, and a girls' school, "Beth Chanah"; both named after the late mother of the Lubavitcher Rebbe שליט"א. The network of primary schools has gained a widespread reputation for the calibre of the students that it produces. Neither are the classrooms empty in the evenings; then they are used by a very active branch of the Chabad Youth Evening Classes for teaching a wide variety of Jewish religious subjects.

Pupils from Beth Chanah School welcome President Shazar.

Adjoining the apartment blocks is the new home of the Toras Emes Yeshivah. Founded originally in Hebron in 1912, it moved later to the Mea Shearim district of Jerusalem. The accommodation and facilities there, however, have long since been inadequate to meet the demands for places at this renowned seat of learning. Since its inception, thousands of students have graduated from this *yeshivah*. They are sought after as Rabbis, *shochetim* and teachers in Israel and in the Diaspora. An important part of the *yeshivah*'s curriculum is the study of *Chabad Chassidus* and

Below and right: Toras Emes Yeshivah, Mea Shearim, Jerusalem—old building.

Bottom: Toras Emes Yeshivah. Almost completed new building adjoining Shikun Chabad.

the students are encouraged to transmit by word and deed their learning in this subject to all with whom they come into contact. This subject is in great demand, too, by the many students who come each evening to learn *gemorrah*, *poskim*, etc., after their normal school studies or work.

The *yeshivah* on its new site provides full-time instruction for some 250 students from many parts of the globe. It includes comfortable dormitories and modern kitchen and dining-room facilities. Its ameni-

Below: Model of the new Toras Emes Yeshivah, Jerusalem.

Opposite: Rabbi C. Glitzenstein and Rabbi E. Wolff welcome visitors to site of the new *yeshivah*.

ties are conducive to the high standard of learning required from its students.

The Shikun Chabad with all its ramifications is only one aspect of the many activities of the Kolel Chabad which was established by the *Alter Rebbe* in 5548 (1788) at the time of the first *Chabad* immigration to *Eretz Yisroel*. Its purpose was to strengthen and to maintain the settlement in the Holy Land by giving assistance to the needy and especially to new immigrants. The Kolel still maintains various aid societies which provide help in obtaining suitable living accommodation, medical care for expectant mothers and the sick, *hachnossas kalloh*, interest-free loans to the needy, etc. It also helps to establish *Chabad* synagogues throughout the country and to provide the *shiurim* held in them.

From 1949 until his recent death, the Kolel Chabad was directed by
Rabbi Azriel Selig Slonim. A descendant of the branch of the *Alter
Rebbe*'s family who settled in Eretz Yisroel 120 years ago, Rabbi Slonim
was born in Hebron and studied at the Tomchei Tmimim Yeshivah
in Lubavitch, Russia. A wise administrator, Rabbi Slonim directed the

Above: Rehov Chabad (Chabad
Street), in the Old City, in which
the Tzemach Tzedek Shul is
situated.

Left: Apartment building project
adjoining Tzemach Tzedek Shul.

Opposite: "Train the child according
to his own way, then even when
he grows old, he will not turn
away from it." (Proverbs 22:6)—
a youthful visitor to the Tzemach
Tzedek Shul.

affairs of the Kolel Chabad with great skill and dignity, winning the respect of all. Since his death, the affairs of the Kolel are being administered by a small committee appointed by the Lubavitcher Rebbe שליט״א; whilst another small committee directs the educational institutions attached to the Shikun Chabad.

One of the ways in which *Chabad*'s long association with the Old City of Jerusalem is noted is by the street which is called Rehov Chabad. In this street near the Western Wall is situated the *shul* named after the *Tzemach Tzedek*, the third Lubavitcher Rebbe, who founded it over one hundred years ago.

Immediately the Old City was regained during the Six-Day War in 1967, the *shul* was found to be the only one there which had not been destroyed, although both the exterior and the interior had been desecrated. The interior was found to be in complete ruin. On the instructions of the Lubavitcher Rebbe שליט״א, the *shul* was temporarily renovated and was in use within a few days. It has since been used regularly for worship. Restoration of the building was immediately undertaken and although far from complete it is already being used for a multiplicity of educational, cultural and social purposes. A permanent exhibition of "*Chabad* over the past 200 years" is planned and will shortly be opened as will be a library and facilities for youth gatherings.

Opposite top: Rabbi S. F. Vogel, Executive Director of Lubavitch Foundation of Great Britain (extreme right), amongst congregants at weekday morning service in the Tzemach Tzedek Shul.

Opposite bottom: Tisha B'Av service.

Left: President Shazar, accompanied by the late Rabbi Azriel Selig Slonim and Rabbi C. Glitzenstein, visits the Tzemach Tzedek Shul shortly after the re-unification of Jerusalem.

Above: The late Rabbi Azriel Selig Slonim.

Work has commenced on a block of flats adjoining the *shul* to house *Chabad* families, so that the street which has borne the name for many years will soon be, literally, a *Chabad* street.

In Jerusalem, as elsewhere, the work of *Chabad* in its *yeshivos*, schools and other institutions is augmented by the less tangible but equally important work in the field of *ooforatzto*—spreading the influence and ideals of *Yiddishkeit* over the widest possible area and so encompassing

Above and below: At the Wall—
Chabadniks put on *Tefillin* with
soldiers.

Opposite: Ohel Yitzchok
Synagogue, Mea Shearim, exterior
and interior.

the largest circle of Jews. It is pleasing and interesting to see now amongst the ranks of *Chabad*, *baalei teshuvah* who join in this work with zeal and with zest not only in Jerusalem but throughout Israel bringing to life the verse: "*For out of Zion shall go forth the Law and the word of the L–rd from Jerusalem.*" (Isaiah 2 : 3).

Some activities at the Tzemach Tzedek Community Centre.

In Israel and throughout the world one will find *Chabadniks* active in matters not specifically associated with *Chabad*. The newly formed Association of Religious Russian Academics in Israel, Shamir, is a good example of this. It is headed by famous physicist, Professor Herman Branover, recently arrived from Riga, seen above with London businessman Mr Peter Kalms, Chairman of the British Friends of Shamir, both active in *Chabad* circles. Shamir has some 400 members, virtually all the religious Russian academics now in Israel. With a central office in Jerusalem and regional offices in other centres, the Association arranges lectures, individual *shiurim*, social and cultural events in order to promote an interest in religion amongst other Russian academics in Israel.

Two-thirds of the Association's budget is devoted to publications. A magazine is to be published every two months and plans are in progress for translations into Russian of religious and philosophical works to be used by the Association members and to be sent to Russia. The Association already has six full-time field workers including an Executive Director.

Above: Professor Branover with newly arrived Russian immigrants.

Right: Part of the audience at a lecture given under the auspices of Shamir.

Chabad House

It is not coincidental that this centre in Jerusalem was given the name "House", for it was intended to be, and has become, a home with an ever-open door. Here, every Jew who seeks friendship and, perhaps, a new spiritual dimension finds a ready welcome and immediately feels at home.

Here, too, young people from different countries and a variety of backgrounds are able to meet and listen to lectures and talks given by specialists in various subjects. These talks in many languages cover topics on Judaism at different levels as well as matters of contemporary interest which are discussed from the standpoint of *Torah* and *Chassidus*. Many of these visitors to Chabad House are, for the first time, made aware of the relevance of *Torah* and of spiritual values which are capable of giving content and meaning to their existence.

Classes in Bible, Oral Law, Jewish History, Jewish Thought, *Chassidic* Philosophy, Jewish Art and Hebrew are regular features. There are also discussion groups which are orientated to the special needs of recent immigrants as yet unacclimatised to their new homeland. Many

find it difficult to effect the changeover to a radically different way of life and need someone to whom they can speak openly and freely. In the "House Parents" they find sympathetic listeners and capable advisers.

But Chabad House serves not only those who have come as immigrants; there are also groups and facilities for visitors to *Eretz Yisroel*. These cultural activities are augmented by social functions consisting of spontaneous gatherings and special celebrations to mark the various Jewish and *Chassidic* festivals. *Onegei Shabbat* and *melavei malka* are held at Chabad House and guests are accommodated for *Shabbosos* and the Festivals in private homes so that they can savour at first-hand an authentic Jewish atmosphere.

A lending library, established at the instigation of the Lubavitcher Rebbe שליט״א, has some 2000 volumes on a wide variety of Jewish and religious subjects. The library also supplies religious requisites such as *Tefillin* and *Mezuzos*.

Extrovert as always, *Chabad Chassidim* regularly visit the Absorption Centres and Universities to meet new immigrants and students. Instruction and talks on a wide variety of Jewish topics are sponsored by the "House" in Absorption Centres, Schools, Colleges, Universities, Youth Organisations and Women's Clubs.

Groups at Chabad House.

Since it was started a little over a year ago, youngsters and adults at the rate of about 1000 a month have visited Jerusalem's Chabad House. Some have been stimulated to make a complete return to their cultural origins and heritage; others have succeeded, as a start, in rekindling the Divine spark buried deep within them. Young men have received the impetus to enter *yeshivah* and young women have felt the need to enter similar establishments of learning for women. Some have succeeded in bringing about a change in their parents' homes where life is now being led in conformity with Jewish Law and tradition. Many even brought their parents to see for themselves what Chabad House has to offer.

Few leave the "House" without a refreshed faith in G–d and a *Chassidic* sense of joy in life. This is reflected in the many expressions of gratitude and appreciation which are received from Jews in all walks of life and representing every shade of ideological conviction, both in Israel and in the Diaspora.

A social evening at Chabad House.

Kfar Chabad

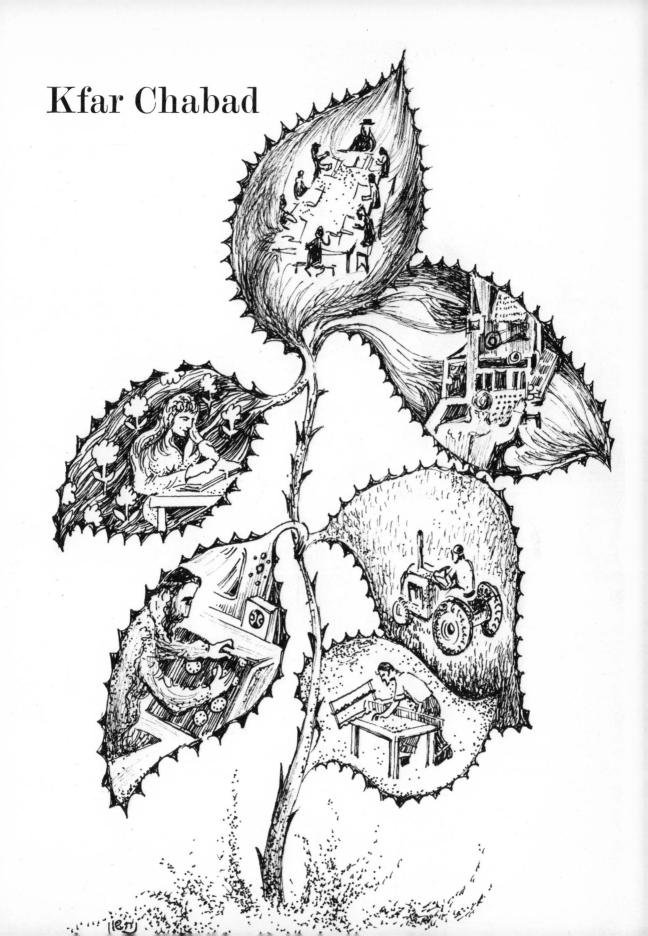

Shalom Aleichem

Israel is a land of desert and burning heat, of sea and of flowers, of snow and of mountains; of bustling cities, humming kibbutzim *and quiet villages. The variety of the land is mirrored in its people, who, be they* sabras *or immigrants, rich or poor, old or young, live together in this little country, and, by doing so, vivify its existence despite its many surrounding enemies and the world.*

Surely something else unites these people of many nationalities, besides the land in which they live.

If not, then how are we able to explain the deep happiness we feel upon seeing a newly arrived Russian immigrant welcomed and embraced by long-lost family and friends? Their language and their culture is completely foreign to us, and yet the bond we share with them is there—albeit tacit.

If not this common bond, then from whence comes the feeling of something shared and understood, communicated through the melodies wafted on the still air of a Shabbos *night?*

Shalom Aleichem—*though you come from desert and the heat, or from the sea, from mountains and the snow.*

Shalom Aleichem—*though you come from bustling cities, worlds apart from the simplicity of the* Kfar.

We are all part of one another: one soul, transcending languages, cultures—all plurality.

The body divides, the soul unites.

"Love your fellow as yourself"—a compelling injunction to reveal in every being the sown seeds of empathy—despite the differences. . . .

The above poem was written by Shloime Levin, formerly of South Africa and at present studying at Kfar Chabad, and his wife Lindy.

The bus from Tel Aviv to Jerusalem does not go into the village itself; but the walk from the bus-stop along the road leading to the village is not long.

Kfar Chabad, the first *Chabad* village in Israel, has several synagogues, a large *yeshivah*, a girls' seminary, day schools, vocational schools, a large youth centre and a brand-new immigrant hostel.

The villagers are, at first sight, unprepossessing. Ordinary people living ordinary lives. Like their counterparts elsewhere they are concerned with the day-to-day events that affect them and their families.

And yet in a land where achievement is no novelty, where communal success stories are commonplace, Kfar Chabad has won universal acclaim.

What is there so special about this village which has grown into a small township? What about it attracts frequent visits not only from the

Kfar Chabad—aerial view.

leaders of Israel but from so many visitors from abroad? What makes its inhabitants beloved by people throughout Israel?

What, in fact, is different about Kfar Chabad? For, assuredly, it is different.

Its difference lies in that its appearance belies the truth. For despite the haphazard building and the casual appearance of the villagers Kfar Chabad is a model of planning.

From the day that the rubble was cleared to make way for the first homes it has grown in accordance with a master plan that has made it a byword in Israel. It was to be a village for Jews who, whilst carrying

out their ordinary labours and professions and participating in the building-up of the land, were intent on living their personal lives in accordance with their strict religious standards in an environment which was conducive to it. But without being a ghetto. For Kfar Chabad was to be, too, a centre to which people would come for a day, a week or years, to learn and to taste and experience the true spirit of *Chabad Chassidus* in practice. Just as importantly, it was to be a centre from which the villagers would go out to every part of Israel to share with every other Jew the teachings of *Chabad* with the warmth and friendship which are its hallmark.

Early agricultural settlers.

In 1949, seventy-four *Chabad* families, new immigrants from Russia, had been directed by the late Lubavitcher Rebbe, Rabbi Joseph Isaac Schneersohn, to settle in the Lod Valley, where the Jewish National Fund had allotted them 600 acres.

Breeding turkeys.

The *Jewish Observer* wrote later: "There were several noteworthy aspects of this *aliyah*. The *Chabad* members refused all offers of help from religious and political organisations; they insisted on going on the land, adapting themselves to modern agricultural methods while at the same time scorning modern *kibbutznik* dress. . . . To them it was a point of honour to live as they taught. This meant subsisting only on what they earned by their own toil."

The Russians were joined later by immigrants from North Africa who were quickly integrated, setting the only pattern that *Chabad* understands: Jews are Jews.

It is not too difficult to build a village on paper, especially in retrospect. In practice, as a day-to-day endeavour, it does not come so easily. Master plans need master executives and this applies especially to a venture like Kfar Chabad where many of the buildings and institutions can truthfully be said to have been built as much of heart as of bricks and mortar.

The history of Kfar Chabad abounds with such master executives. In an organisation such as *Chabad*, where every worker is of major importance, it is particularly invidious to mention some by name, but no one would expect a history of Kfar Chabad, however brief, not to mention Rabbi Pinchas Althaus. The second wing of the new *yeshivah* complex was called "Pinchas House" in remembrance of this wonderful *Chassid* and there is hardly an aspect of the growth of Kfar Chabad with which he was not actively connected and involved. Government ministers, Knesset members, Jewish Agency officials and the villagers all fondly remember Reb Pinchas. He was loved by all and loved everyone.

In 1973 Kfar Chabad continues to grow. Almost a quarter of a century after its inception the houses and institutions have changed beyond recognition. Only the original concept of *Torah*, *ahavas Yisroel* and *avodah* remains unchanged.

We hope that the reader who visits Kfar Chabad with us through this chapter will sense the achievement and purpose of this first *Chabad* village.

The first building to be erected in the new village was a *yeshivah* where the children of the first settlers could study and be educated in the *Chabad* manner. In the evenings, at the end of a day's work in the fields or factory, the large *Beis Hamedrash* at the *yeshivah* became filled with the villagers studying, in small groups, *Gemorrah* or a chapter of *Tanya* or a *maamar* of *Chassidus*.

Top: Early settlers in first *yeshivah* at Kfar Chabad.
Bottom: New *yeshivah* complex.

Above and below: Students from all over the world learning in the new *yeshivah* at Kfar Chabad.

Today the *baalei battim* have their own *batei medrashim* for study and the new *yeshivah* complex houses over 300 students from countries throughout the world who have come to study at one of the acknowledged great centres of learning in *Eretz Yisroel*. The graduates of the *yeshivah* are in great demand as Rabbis and teachers both in Israel and the Diaspora but the primary aspect of learning at the *yeshivah*, as with all *Chabad* learning, is an approach to life; the *Chabad derech*. To inculcate in the students a correct approach to G–d and to their fellow Jew.

Left: Learning in solitude.

Top: Mrs. Golda Meir.

Above: General Narkis.

Below: Chief Rabbi Unterman visits the *yeshivah*.

Opposite: Midnight rendezvous for learning.

Above: A knotty problem?

Below left: A student amongst his *seforim.*

Centre and opposite page: Classes in the special preparatory course and programme.

Below right: On leave. A temporary return from tank to *Talmud.*

To cater for the influx of young men from the Diaspora who come to Kfar Chabad with little basic Jewish learning, the *yeshivah* has set up a special preparatory course and programme. Attracted by the honest intellectual approach of *Chabad* these young men, many of them university graduates, most with only a limited knowledge of their Jewish heritage, come to discover their origins and their faith. The programme, under the direction of experienced teachers in this field, consists of instruction in the basic tenets of Judaism together with *Chabad* philosophy. These students mix with their more advanced colleagues in the *yeshivah* at *farbrengens* and other social activities and are in this way integrated into an observant society.

The age old discussion of a difficult *gemorrah*.

Yet another category of young men is provided for by the vocational schools which are a special feature of Kfar Chabad. It was realised from the outset that not all the young men, whether the children of the original settlers or new immigrants, would be suitable for the advanced studies conducted at the *yeshivah* and that these young people would need to receive a vocational training. So, in 1954 a Carpentry School was opened to provide training in woodwork and carpentry. This was soon followed in 1955 by an Agriculture School. These two schools flourished, attracting many pupils both from the *Kfar* and outside.

Modern techniques at the carpentry school.

MURDER!

Following the murder of the five students, recounted on the following pages, the Lubavitcher Rebbe שליט"א sent ten senior students to augment the work of the Kfar.

Below: The ten students arriving at Lod Airport and (left) poster welcoming their arrival.

In 1955 came a major setback. Five children and a teacher were attacked and murdered by Arab terrorists whilst at evening prayers. All Israel was outraged. The authorities at Kfar Chabad, shocked by the tragedy and mindful of the danger of further infiltration, thought it desirable to close the schools. The Lubavitcher Rebbe שליט״א thought otherwise. In a cable he urged the expansion of the facilities offered by the vocational schools. As a result, within a short time, the Yad Hachamisha School of Printing and Graphic Arts was opened and dedicated to the memory of the five victims of the terrorist attack.

Laying the Printing School foundation stone in memory of the murdered students. The completed school is shown below.

Printing School interior.

Pupils at work in
Vocational Schools.

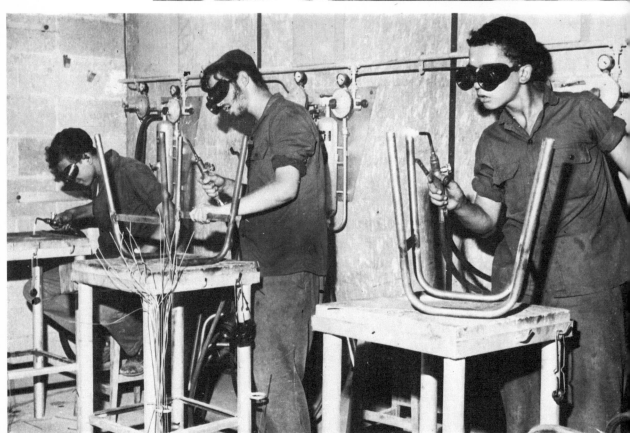

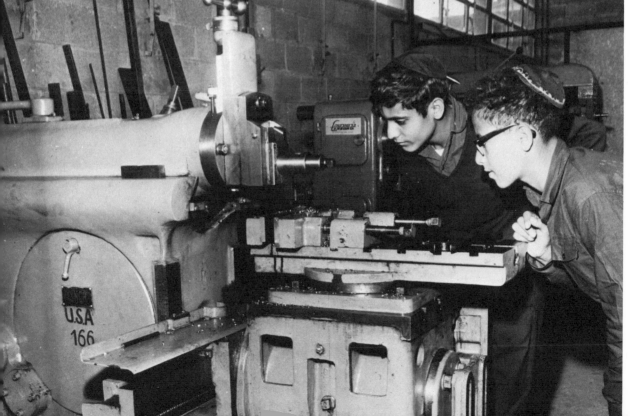

In 1964 a Metal Working School was added. Changes and advancement in the technical and environmental climate of Israel is reflected in the schools. More recently, the Agriculture School has been replaced by one teaching agro-mechanical techniques. A new school for instruction in the design and application of pneumatic equipment and electronics in industry has been added. To cater for the recent influx of immigrants from Georgia and other parts of Russia special vocational classes have been added.

Agro-mechanical School.

To complete the complex of vocational schools which greet the visitor as he enters the village from the road, there are two large buildings which have 100 small dormitories, 20 classrooms and 7 lecture halls. A beautiful modern synagogue was erected in 1965 and all the furniture was made by pupils of the carpentry schools. The printing schools print many of the *seforim* which emanate from *Chabad* in *Eretz Yisroel* and are distributed throughout the world. In addition, orders are fulfilled for many commercial undertakings in Israel.

All the technical training given to the 450 pupils of these vocational schools is under the supervision of the Vocational Training Department of the Ministry of Education.

The technical training given to the pupils is not an end in itself, but is part of an overall system of training in *Torah*. All the youngsters devote half of each working day to religious studies. By the time they graduate, the vocational school students have not only acquired a means of livelihood but are also fully conversant with the basics of *Torah* and *Chassidus* and are imbued with *yiras shomayim*. The trade which the pupil has learnt has been taught from the *Chassidic* standpoint. It is a means to obtain *parnossa* so that one may further one's *Torah* study and fulfil the *mitzvos*; for man does not live by bread alone.

Left: Vocational Schools' dormitories.
Above: Vocational Schools' synagogue; exterior and interior.

The success of the vocational schools can be measured to some extent by the large waiting list of prospective pupils and by the demand for the graduates, who are known to have acquired a high standard of craftsmanship. Perhaps a better indication, however, are the thousands of former students who lead full and useful lives in the communities in which they have settled; lives distinguished by their attachment to *Torah* and *mitzvos* and by their desire to influence their fellow Jews along this path and to help them in every possible way.

The visitor to Kfar Chabad cannot help being impressed at the simple beauty of the Beth Rivkah Schools which provide an education for girls which is a counterpart of that available to the boys. The surrounding landscaping provides a tasteful extension of the well-planned classes, lecture rooms and residential facilities within the school buildings.

Left: Students relaxing on the expansive lawns, which are a feature of the Beth Rivkah Schools.

Below, from top to bottom: Dining Rooms; End of classes for a day; A break in studies.

The Beth Rivkah primary schools provide an elementary education in religious and secular studies for over 400 girls to the age of fourteen, at which time the pupils are streamed between the High School and the vocational schools. The former continue both their religious and secular studies at a higher level. The pupils at the vocational schools, whilst still receiving secular and religious instruction, devote half of their working day to learning dressmaking, wigmaking and laboratory work.

Rabbi Shmuel Haifer, director of Beth Rivkah Schools and Seminary, with students.

Left: Mrs. Golda Meir, Prime Minister of Israel, visiting the Beth Rivkah Schools.

Below: Dressmaking—pattern drawing, cutting and machining.

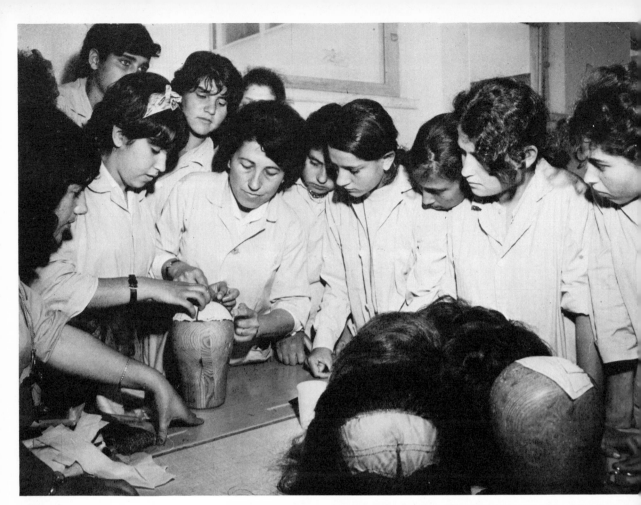

Above: Wigmaking.

Right: Gardening. A useful exercise.

The Teachers Training Seminary provides a two-year course for graduates from the High School and for girls of similar educational standard from countries abroad, leading on graduation to the State Teachers Certificate. Altogether, girls from over fifty different countries are at present receiving their education at these schools. The pedagogic objective of the Teachers Training Seminary is to prepare its graduates as educators and teachers and, on completion of their course, they are placed as such in *Chabad* schools[1] throughout Israel. There, in addition to teaching, they are able to spread the light and warmth of *Chassidus* in their new environment. More recently, graduates of the Seminary have become teachers at *Chabad* schools in the U.S.A., France and Italy, realising the words of the Lubavitcher Rebbe שליט"א who has said: "The Beth Rivkah Schools must become a spiritual centre not only for Kfar Chabad, not even only for Israel, but for the whole world."

[1] *Chabad* schools here is not used as a term for schools catering for *Chabad* children. Throughout Israel, *Chabad* staff government schools which provide an education for over 8,000 children—see section on schools.

Mrs. Golda Meir visits schools' kitchen.

But it is not only the bright buildings which will impress the visitor to the schools. Even more impressive are the students. They are alert and active like all pupils. Meet them in the classroom, in the gardens, relaxing on the lawn or in their own club. One group may be discussing a chapter of *Tanya*, another a mathematical problem. You may find them excitedly preparing for the annual camp or seriously preparing for a discussion of ideas with a guest group from a *kibbutz*.

Most certainly you will find them happy.

Contrast the light and dark eyed: the understanding light in the eyes of a Yemenite girl, the special thoughtfulness reflected in the eyes of a northern girl. They are, however, strongly united in their special study programmes which, above all, contain the eternal value of Jewish thought in general and *Chassidic* thought in particular.

At Beth Rivkah.

The small dormitories have been attractively designed to provide a
home-from-home atmosphere. The housemothers' task is to foster this
atmosphere. For social activities the girls are organised into groups,
each with a group leader whose duty it is to supervise the educational
development of each girl as well as to create social activities which will
complement the knowledge acquired by the girls in school. Lectures by
guest speakers cover a wide range of topics and problems. Meetings
between the pupils and those from other institutions are a great success.
These meetings often develop into a warm friendship between the girls
and to the spreading of *Torah* enlightenment to groups who were
previously unfamiliar with it.

School orchestra.

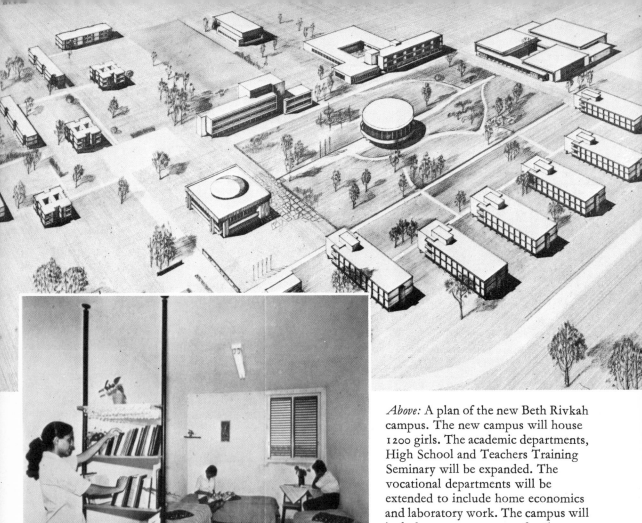

Above: A plan of the new Beth Rivkah campus. The new campus will house 1200 girls. The academic departments, High School and Teachers Training Seminary will be expanded. The vocational departments will be extended to include home economics and laboratory work. The campus will include a new synagogue for the girls, a comprehensive library, lecture halls, a clinic, a swimming pool and accommodation for staff members.

Left: A dormitory.

Opposite: Tefillah.

One cannot fail to feel the spirit of *Chabad* which pervades the schools. *Chassidic* teaching sheds its bright light and influence on all shades, elevating them to a special level. The melodies one hears are *Chabad* melodies and the special atmosphere is even more strongly felt on *Shabbos* and the *Yomim Tovim*.

In short, education at the Beth Rivkah Schools is a spiritual and intellectual preparation for life ahead. Spiritually, to prepare the student for the duty of being a wife and mother within the sacred meaning of those terms. Intellectually, so that wherever she may find herself, she will be equipped to fashion her environment rather than be influenced by it.

One of the newer buildings in Kfar Chabad is the Youth Centre. Opened in 1969 to mark the twentieth anniversary of the founding of Kfar Chabad, it was named "Beth Shazar" in honour of Shneur Zalman Shazar, the President of Israel, himself a Lubavitcher *Chassid*. At last, Kfar Chabad had a suitable venue to hold youth conventions and to welcome, *en masse*, youth from all over Israel and abroad and it was not long before the new addition echoed with voices of the young. Summer conventions, winter reunions and weekend visits by the young of all shades of religious observance eager to meet again with their friends from *Chabad*.

Below: Beth Shazar—a venue for a variety of important occasions. Inset: President and Mrs. Shazar visit the synagogue at Beth Shazar.

Kfar Chabad was delighted when the Jewish Agency decided to build there a hostel to accommodate observant new immigrants until they had found or prepared their permanent homes in Israel. And the new immigrants are delighted at the warm welcome they receive from the villagers.

A few shops, the post office, the clinic, the kindergartens and you may think that you have completed your tour and that you have seen everything.

You would be wrong. You must come again and see more and different things.

For the face of Kfar Chabad changes with the seasons of the year.

New immigrants' hostel at Kfar Chabad.

Above: Deputy Mayor Rothenburg of New York on a visit to the *Kfar*.

Top right: Former Chief Rabbi Nissim at a *Kfar* celebration.

Right: Mr. Israel Yeshayahu.

Right: Mayor Lindsay of New York with Mrs. Lindsay meet Mayor Maidenchik of Kfar Chabad during a visit there.

Below and bottom: Chanukah celebrations.

The approach of *Pesach* sees the baking of *shemura matzos*—and visits by busloads of schoolchildren from near and far to watch the baking, to learn its significance and to return home carrying a sample for use at their own *Seder* table. Last year some 6,000 children visited Kfar Chabad in the weeks before *Pesach* and left knowing far more about this particular *mitzvah* and its relevance to them.

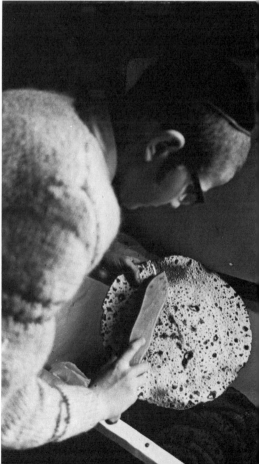

Other *yomim tovim*—*Chanukah, Purim, Shovuos, Succos*—change the scene each in its particular way. *Simchas Torah* at Kfar Chabad is an unforgettable experience.

The *Chassidic* festivals, *Yud tes Kislev, Yud Shevat, Yud beis Tammuz*, see hundreds of visitors joining the *Chassidim* in a spirited enjoyment of these special occasions; but if these occasions are times of joyousness they are, in *Chabad* style, times for learning too and times for strengthening one's bonds with G–d.

Concerts by the schools' orchestras, exhibitions on various topics, lectures, *farbrengens*, festivals of music all add their special flavour to this special village.

Since 1967 Kfar Chabad has been one of the venues, too, for the *Barmitzvah* celebrations arranged by *Chabad* for war orphans.

Simchas Torah at Kfar Chabad.

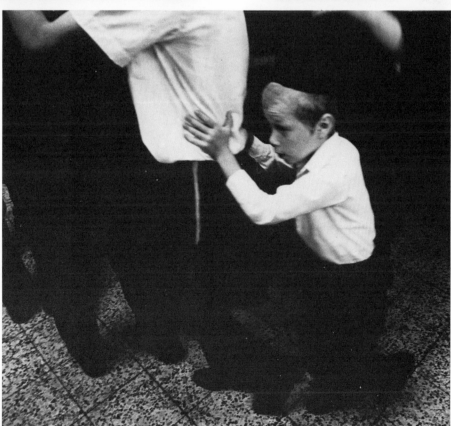

Simchas Torah at Kfar Chabad.

And amidst all this the normal life of the village goes on. The villagers have the usual personal joys and sorrows, children are born, grow up, study, work and marry. Our villagers, however, are not introverts—*Chabad Chassidim* cannot be—for they are part of an outward-looking movement. Wherever you are in Israel you will meet them, together with their colleagues from other centres, participating in the campaigns for which *Chabad* is famous and which are portrayed elsewhere in this volume.

But their home, their family life, is in the village which after more than two decades holds a special distinction. It is the only village in Israel in which there is no case registered of a villager leaving.

As a recent publication issued by the Government says: "In Israel there are many *kibbutzim*, many villages, many towns. There is only one Kfar Chabad."

Outpatients' clinic.

Above: The famous generator at Kfar Chabad which supplies electricity to the village on *Shabbosos* and *Yomim Tovim* to ensure that the villagers do not benefit from other Jews' labours on forbidden occasions. The electricity consumed is still metered and paid for to the Electricity Authority.

Left: Early morning prayers.

Lively discussion

Silent prayer.

A new grandchild?

A new gift?

Left: Rabbi Avrohom Parish who, until his death, was the Rebbe's personal emissary in *Eretz Yisroel.*

Below: A *halachic* discussion— or just reminiscing?

Opposite: Kibbutzniks at discussions on arrival at Kfar Chabad for a week-end visit.

Children at play.

Mesibos Shabbos group parade.

The Wedding

The different faces of the Mayor of Kfar Chabad

Above: Private *Talmudic* study with sons.   *Below:* With distinguished visitors to Beth Shazar.

Left: Public *farbrengen.*

Below: Private reunion.

Above and right: Pursuing his occupation as train driver.

Opposite top: A busman's holiday—around the Kfar on a scooter.

Opposite bottom: Discussing the affairs of the community.

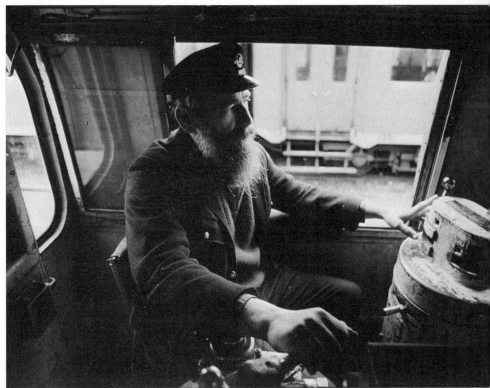

A few of the famous visitors to Kfar Chabad

Below: World-famous *Talmudist* Rabbi Zevin (right) with
Chief Rabbi Unterman.

Opposite top: Prime Minister Mrs. Golda Meir and newly
arrived pupils at the Talmud Torah.

Opposite bottom left: The late Rabbi Pinchas Althaus with
Chief Rabbi Unterman.

Opposite bottom right: General "Arik" Sharon joins festivities.

Above: English visitors Mr. Arnold Lee and Mr. Henry Lewis at one of the vocational schools.

Right: The late Mr. Levi Eshkol, then Prime Minister of Israel, at the *Kfar*.

Above: Mr. Moshe Sharett, then Prime Minister of Israel, with early settlers.

Left: Mr. Aron Becker chats with apprentices at a vocational school.

Above: Mr. Menachem Begin (extreme right) in festive mood.

Opposite top: Mr. Meyer Weisgal (centre), president of the Weitzman Institute, and Chief Rabbi Unterman.

Opposite bottom: Leading personalities visiting Kfar Chabad.

Personally

BY DVORAH RABINOWITZ

Ever since we came to Israel I had wanted to participate in some of the festivities at Kfar Chabad, the village established by Lubavitch *Chassidim*. The event that has attracted thousands of visitors and brings together most of the *Chassidim* from every part of the country and from every walk of life is the celebration held on the 19th day of *Kislev*. This celebration commemorates the release in 1798 of the founder of the movement, Rabbi Shneur Zalman, from a St Petersburg prison. This year I was determined to attend the festivities.

Fortunately, we have a distant relative living in Kfar Chabad who invited me to come early in the afternoon so that I could visit the village and obtain a good seat in the main synagogue where the official celebration took place.

On a privately guided tour, I visited the many schools maintained by the 200 families who live in the *Kfar*. The schools are under the supervision of the Religious Department of the Ministry of Education, and some have dormitories for the out-of-town students. There are printing and carpentry vocational schools for boys, vocational schools for girls where sewing and wigmaking are the specialities, a girls' Teachers Training Seminary, a *yeshivah ketanah*, a *yeshivah gedoloh*, a *kolel* and a magnificent new youth centre in the name of Israel's President Zalman Shazar, the most illustrious Lubavitch *Chassid* in Israel.

By the time I came to the synagogue, the one row of seats reserved for the women was already taken and I had to stand on a bench. In the men's section, long tables were set up the entire centre length of the synagogue, and rising on each side were benches arranged in amphitheatre style, the last rows reaching as high as the windows. Only the early arrivals found seats at the tables, and hundreds of others stood on the benches—more could be accommodated that way.

On the *bimah* was a long table for the distinguished visitors, among whom were President Shazar, Rabbi S. Zevin, editor of the *Talmudic Encyclopedia*, revered rabbis and other leading personalities. Just in front of the *Aron Hakodesh*, which was covered with a curtain, sat the famous *Chabad* choir, comprising about ten men in their middle years with flowing beards and magnificent voices, who not only rendered special selections, but led the group singing.

When the Presidential car arrived, the roar was so loud that it filled the air and penetrated into the synagogue. The choir sang and everyone joined in—the men standing on the benches were dancing up and down in place, the only direction permitted by the crowded conditions! Then one of the *Chassidim* on the *bimah* flung off his jacket, threw it up on the rafters and began to dance—with much grace and evident joy—accompanied by the rhythmic clapping and singing of every *Chassid* in the synagogue.

Outside, the loudspeakers blared forth the singing and the clapping,

and through the windows I could see the circles of dancers. But it was the *Chassid* dancing in front of the *Aron Hakodesh* who captured my attention, and my heart danced with him.

Temporarily, the singing and dancing ended (it eventually continued until the early morning hours) as the formal programme began with greetings and speeches from the learned guests on the significance of the teachings of Rabbi Schneerson, and on how to carry on his tradition of knowledge and joy in the *Torah* and love for our fellow Jews.

Would that the Lubavitcher Rebbe, whose influence is so vast, find ways to inculcate the *Chassidic* credo of understanding and genuine love for fellow Jews, so that it be practised and observed by our own people from this day forth!

(Reprinted from the monthly magazine *The Mizrachi Woman of America*).

Schools

Newly arrived immigrant from Rumania
learns blessing on eating bread at a *Chabad* school.

In education as in everything else *Chabad* does not seek to isolate itself but, on the contrary, always seeks to extend its influence to as large and varied a sphere as possible.

It was for this reason that in 1952 when *Chabad* in Israel embarked on a schools' programme, their schools became part of the Government education system under the supervision of the Religious Department of the Ministry of Education.

Since 1952 the *Chabad* schools have grown into a network providing a religious and secular education for some 8,000 children from the town of Teanach in the north to Brosh in the Negev. The network continues to grow both in numbers and scope. The pupils, who come from vastly varied social and religious backgrounds, receive a secular education as laid down by the Ministry of Education plus an intensive religious education which lays great stress on personal conduct, attitudes and the practice of religion as a way of life. The cost of this additional tuition

Elementary school, Lod.

as well as the additional cost of providing separate classes for boys and girls over five years of age are borne by *Chabad*. All the teachers at these schools are graduates of *Chabad yeshivos* and Teachers' Training Seminaries. The children's education does not finish at the close of school; clubs, camps, outings, extra-curricular studies are provided by the teachers after school hours and during holiday periods. By means of teachers/parents committees, the parents are brought into the excellent atmosphere which prevails in all the schools and a large measure of success has been achieved in bringing many of the parents closer to religious practice and observance through the children. It is difficult for parents to resist extending into their own homes an atmosphere which visibly gives their children great happiness.

The success which has been achieved is best illustrated by the school at Ir-ganim, a district near Jerusalem. This school started in 1959 with 38 pupils and a handful of workers. By 1962, the roll had reached 675.

Elementary school, Jaffa.

Children transferred from other schools; immigrants aware of the reputation of *Chabad* in the country of their origin were happy to enrol their children in a *Chabad* school in their new homeland. By 1964 the numbers had reached 1,700 and today some 3,000 pupils receive instruction in an establishment which includes kindergarten, day-centre schools and post-graduate classes. Despite overcrowding, which is mainly due to the difficulty in keeping pace with the new enrolments, the standard of education is very high and the influence which the school has had on the neighbourhood is immense.

The school in Ir-ganim is exceptional in its growth; not every school has such a wide catchment area and the schools within the network obviously differ in other respects too. But all the schools have at least one thing in common—a dedicated staff who are interested in and concerned with the personal and spiritual welfare of each pupil.

Elementary school, Bat Yam.

Kiryat Gat School welcomes a visit from
Mr. Yigal Allon, Deputy Prime Minister.

191

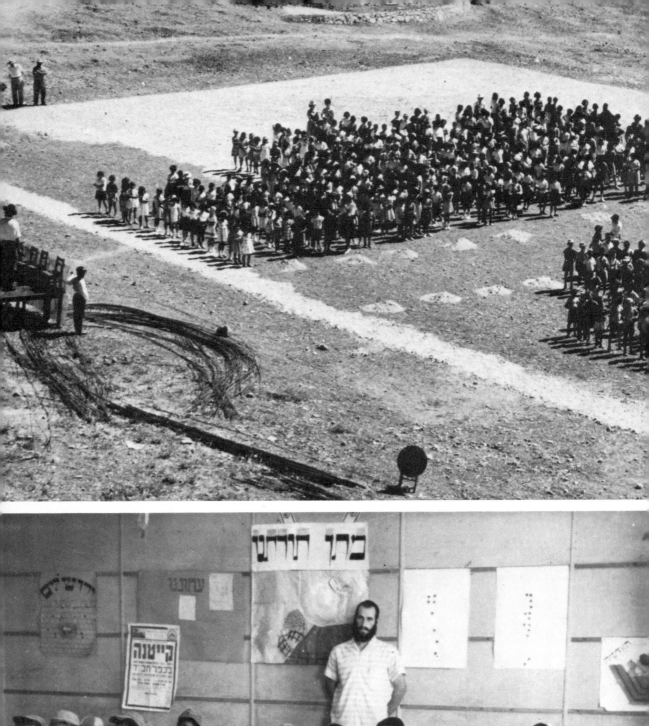

Above: School assembly.

Left and right: In class.

stive occasion at Ir-ganim.

Folk dancing lessons.

Girls class of Ir-ganim. *Opposite:* Beth Chanah School.

Six Days
and its
Aftermath

War orphans at *Chanukah* party at Kfar Chabad.

The effect of the Six-Day War on the religious outlook and life of Jews in Israel—and the Diaspora—has been the subject of much speculation. The "is" and "the might have been" have been endlessly discussed.

Was the spiritual spark of that moment in Jewish history insufficiently harnessed or was it, at the outset, only a momentary emotional outburst? Were the events of that hot June really miracles (or as one senior army officer told the writer "most irrational") or just the inevitable result of careful planning and military prowess? Were the hardened veterans who danced and cried and prayed at The Wall prompted only by pride at the re-unification of Jerusalem (and if so, why the prayers?) or was this the emergence of the eternal soul of the Jew—the holy spark in each of us that oft-times becomes a little tarnished and over-submerged in our day-to-day life.

Whatever the reason, whatever our view, few could help but be stirred by the events of that wonderful week in 1967; few could help but be concerned at the happenings in the days and weeks that preceded it. In those weeks of high tension, the Lubavitcher Rebbe שליט״א advised his followers to ignore the advice to leave Israel given by many neutral countries to their nationals. The Rebbe observed: "Israel's Guardian is surely not asleep."

Like their counterparts throughout Israel, many *Chabadniks* left their jobs or studies to re-join their units. The newspaper and television reports from the battlefronts carried their full quota about *Chassidim* in *Taleisim* and *Tefillin* praying at the side of their tanks or in other theatres of war.

At this time, too, just before the outbreak of the Six-Day War, the Lubavitcher Rebbe instructed the Lubavitch Youth Organisation ("Youth" here being an estate of mind rather than age!) in Israel and throughout the world to initiate an active *Tefillin* campaign, to see that Jews observe the *mitzvah* of *Tefillin*, adding that it is also a means of ensuring Divine protection against Israel's enemies.

The war was fought and the war was won.

Israel's victory brought joy and exhilaration to the Jewish people throughout the world. Inevitably, it also brought tragedy to hundreds of Israeli children whose fathers died so that Israel might live.

The Rebbe immediately instructed his *Chassidim* that, whilst the Israeli Government supported these children within the framework of the legislation, it was necessary that strenuous efforts be made to help fill the place of their fathers in spiritual matters, as all this now devolved on their busy mothers.

As a result of these instructions, War Orphan Committees were established by *Chabad* wherever it is represented throughout the world. The funds raised by these Committees are being used to implement the plans to care for the war orphans' education, to provide them with clothes, holidays and toys, and to provide assistance where needed.

Barmitzvah celebrations are held at Kfar Chabad and Holy Days are commemorated in some practical form.

The Chabad War Orphan activities are acclaimed by every section of the community in Israel.

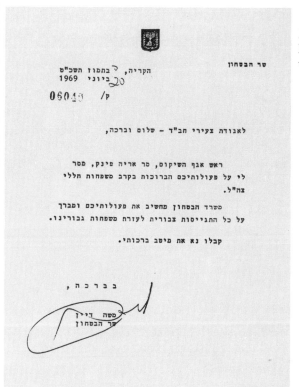

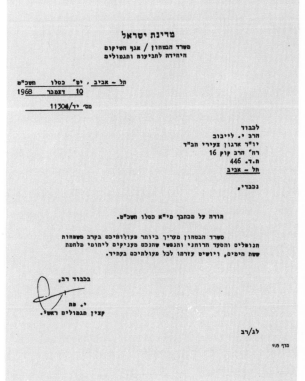

Left: Letter from Moshe Dayan, Israel Defence Minister, commending *Chabad*'s work for war orphans.

Right: Letter from Israel Defence Ministry to the Lubavitch Organisation for War Orphans: "The Defence Ministry greatly values your work for the families of those fallen in the war, and the spiritual help which you give to the orphans of the Six-Day War. It will give its assistance to all your future efforts."

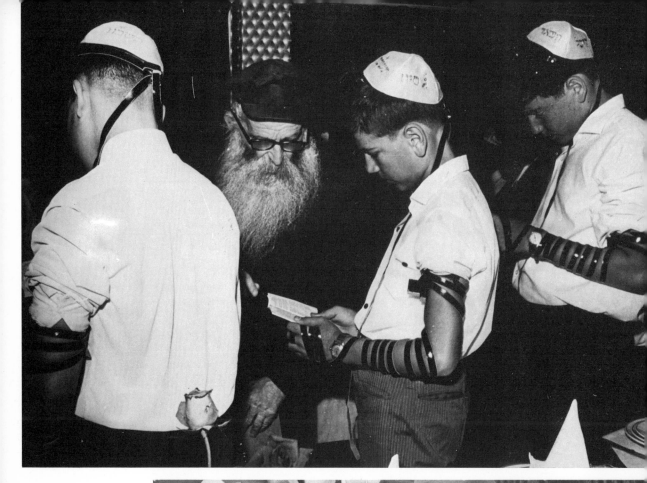

Top and right: War orphan *Barmitzvah* celebrants.

Opposite: A senior army officer puts on *Tefillin* at war orphans *Barmitzvah* celebrations.

204

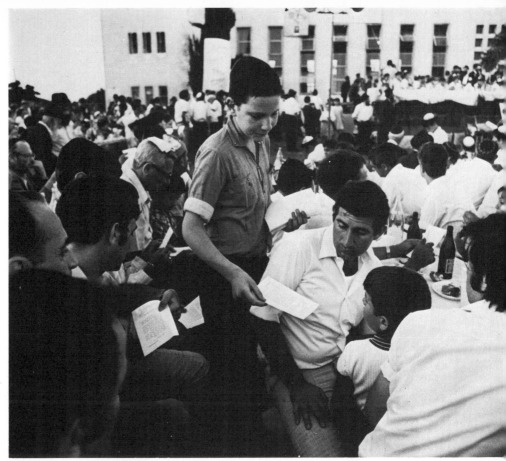

Right: Visitors to *Barmitzvah* celebrations.

Below: 43 boys, orphans of the Six-Day War and subsequent hostilities, at *Barmitzvah* celebrations attended by more than 5000 guests.

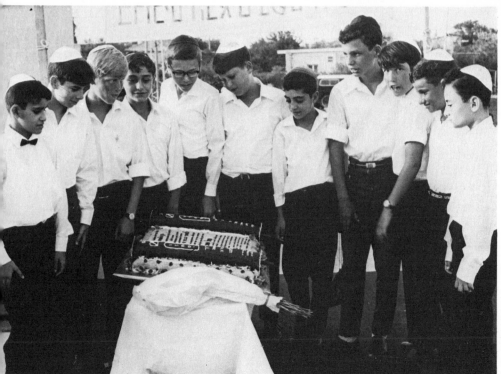

Above: Generals greet young participants.

Left: The boys view the birthday cake.

Above: General Hod and General Ze'evi with other senior officers.
Below: Kfar Chabad entertains war orphan *Barmitzvah* celebrants.

Above: "*Lechayim*".

Opposite top: Army chiefs dancing with *Barmitzvah* celebrants.

Opposite bottom: *Chassidim* and celebrants dancing together.

Hebrew text on cake: שמחת בת מצוה

Above: President
[S]hazar and General
[R]abbi Goren at
[c]elebrations for
[g]irls.

Opposite: The
[g]enerals dance.

[R]ight: President
[S]hazar welcomes
[w]ar orphan
[b]armitzvah cele-
[b]rants in his office,
[19]70.

Above and left:
Chanukah celebrations.

Opposite: Festivities at Kfar
Chabad

Chanukah 1972. Party for war orphans attended by Mayor Lindsay of New York.

Below: Mrs. Shifra Golombovitz with her family.

Mrs Shifra Golombovitz, who plays a special role
in both the *Tefillin* and the War Orphans'
campaigns, at girls' birthday celebrations.[1]

[1] See "CHALLENGE"—an encounter with Lubavitch-Chabad
pp. 147 to 150.

Nachalat
Har Chabad

Aerial view.

On the directive of the Lubavitcher Rebbe שליט״א , Nachalat Har Chabad was established at Kiryat Malachi in 1969. It was specifically intended to cope with an influx of *Chabad Chassidim* from abroad. More recently, large numbers of newly arrived immigrants from Russia have settled there.

Some 400 families are housed in a modern apartment-block complex with its own shopping centre and many other amenities.

Like its counterpart at Kfar Chabad, the newer village has its own schools, *yeshivah* and vocational schools and plans are in being to add other educational facilities and a medical centre.

Factories for diamond polishing, the manufacture of textiles and allied products have been established to aid the economy and to provide employment for the villagers.

Synagogues which are also venues for *shiurim* and youth activities have been erected and are put to good use.

By catering in this way for the material, spiritual and recreational needs of the villagers the newly arrived immigrants are speedily and happily integrated into their new environment without interfering with their time-honoured traditions and customs.

Some of the best students from other *Chabad yeshivos* were encouraged to move to Nachalat Har Chabad where they are now living. They are learning at the newly established *Kolel* there and are helping to spread *Yiddishkeit* in the surrounding areas.

Purim celebrations.

Yud Kislev farbrengen at Nachalat Har Chabad.

Above: Apartment building with playground in forefront.

Opposite: Residents of Nachalat Har Chabad joyously carry and receive two *Sifrei Torah* sent to them from New York by the Lubavitcher Rebbe שליט״א.

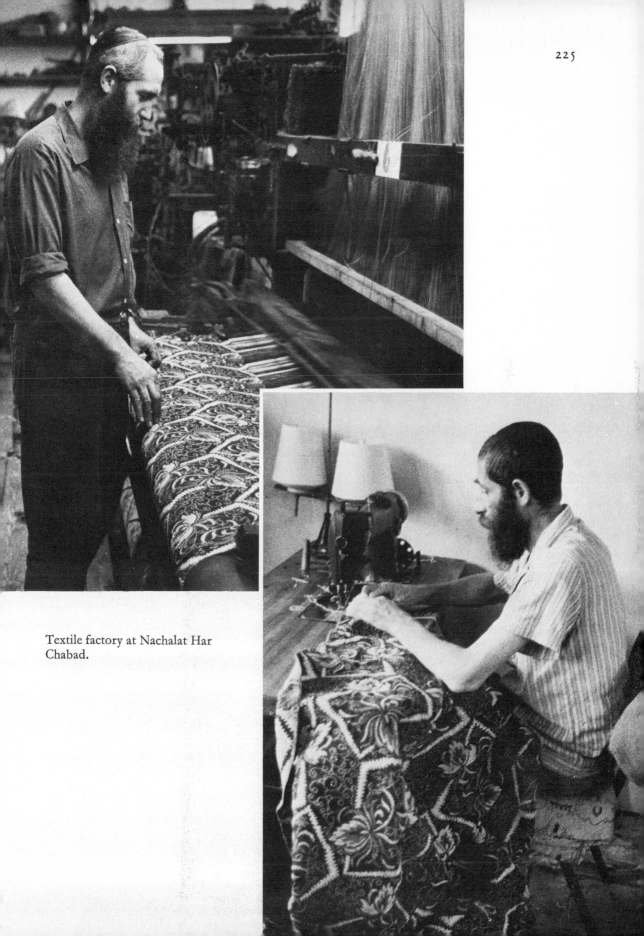

225

Textile factory at Nachalat Har
Chabad.

Above: Diamond polishing—one of the industries established at Nachalat Har Chabad.

Opposite: New immigrants from Bukhara participate in a *shiur* after a day's work.

Opposite: *Yud Beis Tammuz farbrengen.*

Right: Afternoon prayer at *Chabad* school.

Below: Family gathering.

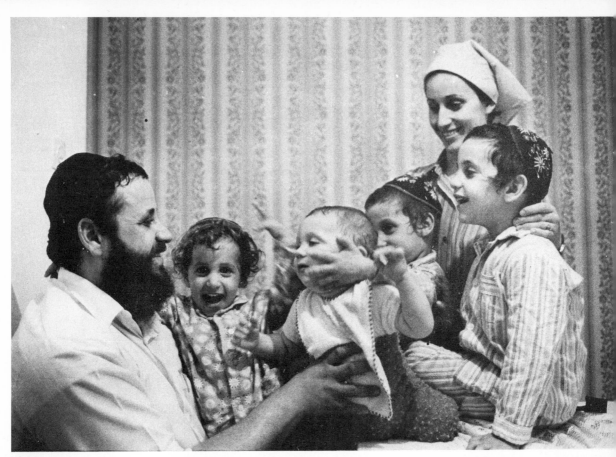

pposite top: Rabbi Berke Wolff, a
bra Chabadnik who settled in
achalat Har Chabad with his wife
d four sons to help rehabilitate
w Russian immigrants.

pposite bottom: Several generations
immigrant family from Georgia
settled in new *Chabad* village.

bove and right: Russian immigrants
d freedom and happiness in
eir new surroundings.

Above: Afternoon classes at *Chabad* school.
Right: Lag B'Omer outing.
Below: Evening *shiur* in synagogue.
Opposite: Russian immigrants.

Recently arrived immigrants from Georgia now happily
settled in Nachalat Har Chabad.

Chabad help to integrate old friends

The association between the Bukharan community and the Holy Land began almost eighty years ago. In 1895, Bukharan Jews under the leadership of Rabbis from Samarkand and Tashkent, such as Chief Rabbi Abraham Talmudy who became the Rabbi of the Bukharan suburb of Jerusalem, began to settle in *Eretz Yisroel*.

The association between *Chabad* and the Bukharan community had begun earlier.

The fifth Lubavitcher Rebbe, Rabbi Sholom Dovber, had sent Rabbis and teachers to Bukhara in order to teach and guide the local Jews who were searching for the word of G–d and were interested and eager to learn *Torah*. Among the earliest immigrants from Bukhara were Rabbi Shlomo Leib Eliezrov and Rabbi Abraham Chaim Naeh who earlier had been sent by Rabbi Sholom Dovber from *Eretz Yisroel* to Bukhara for this express purpose. These two Rabbis were the central personalities in a far reaching programme to teach and demonstrate to the Bukharan community a correct approach to Jewish life. They also encouraged the Bukharan Jews to establish places of learning in order to produce from their own ranks Rabbis, teachers and *shochetim*; spiritual leaders who in turn imbued their followers with a love of G–d and of Judaism strong enough to withstand and overcome the tremendous changes and difficult circumstances which overtook their community.

In 1920 the Red Army conquered Bukhara and, in common with their co-religionists throughout the Soviet Union, the Bukharan Jews began to experience pressures which were to increase over the years. Despite this, and the extreme opposition to the teaching and practice of their religion, they remained loyal to the tenets of their faith.

Bukharan immigrants at *shiurim* at Chabad
Yeshivah in Rishon le Zion.

Rabbi Shlomo Leib Eliezrov.

Morning prayers at *yeshivah*

Between 1927 and 1931 some of them managed to cross the Soviet and Persian borders, finding their way to *Eretz Yisroel*. So strong was their desire to settle in the Holy Land, that they were not deterred by the risks or by the sufferings which ensued if they were caught.

From 1932 the persecution of Jews was intensified both on communal and personal levels; synagogues and places of learning were closed and personal attacks on Jews became more frequent. The Bukharan Jews did not despair. Fortified by their strong belief they continued to teach and practise secretly, and planned constantly to escape at the first opportunity to the Holy Land to live a true Jewish life in freedom.

No large emigration of Bukharan Jews was possible until recent years, but their resolve was not weakened by over three decades of persecution and imprisonment for no other crimes than being Jewish and wishing to remain so. They withstood all attempts by the Government to intimidate them and continued to raise generations of loyal and G–d-fearing Jews.

The Bukharan community was among the first to acknowledge the diligent, self-sacrificing work of the *Chabad* emissaries sent first by Rabbi Sholom Dovber and later by his son the late Lubavitcher Rebbe, Rabbi Joseph Isaac Schneersohn. These *Chabad Chassidim* helped this segment of Jewry to establish and maintain their work in the field of religious education and practice.

It came as no surprise, therefore, that as soon as Bukharan Jews began to arrive in *Eretz Yisroel* in significant numbers, *Chabad* helped them to satisfy their thirst for *Torah* study by providing facilities for them at the Chabad Yeshivah at Rishon le Zion. Several months after the construction of a new wing to accommodate the Bukharan students, the *yeshivah*'s two large buildings were being used by some 150 students

Above: Rabbi Zevulin Labiov and, on his right, Rabbi Avrohom Chaim Ladayev. Both Rabbi Zevulin Labiov (b. 1901) and Rabbi Avrohom Ladayev (b. 1886) had early *Chabad* associations, studying under Rabbi Simcha Gorodetski. They spent long terms in prison and experienced great suffering at the hands of the Russians for their work in many fields of strengthening *Yiddishkeit* and providing means to learn and practise it. In *Eretz Yisroel*, Rabbi Labiov and Rabbi Ladayev still hold important positions within the Bukharan community. Rabbi Ladayev now lives in Natanya where he gives a daily *shiur* in *Tanya* to Bukharan immigrants in the Bukharan *shul* there.

Left: Rabbi Rafael Chodaitov was born in Kaukund in 1898 and until 1910 learned in *Talmud Torah* there. In 1910 he visited Jerusalem together with his parents and learned for a while at Rehovot before returning to Bukhara. Following pogroms, he moved in 1917 to Samarkand where he continued learning for two years at *yeshivah*. From then on he devoted his life to assisting his fellow Jews. His association with *Chabad* started in 1928. During the Second World War, when tens of thousands of Jews from Eastern Europe fled to Bukhara, Rabbi Chodaitov was in the forefront of those arranging and offering them succour. He is particularly well known for his *mesiras nefesh* in matters relating to the erection and maintenance of *mikvaos* and the establishment of underground *chadorim* for Bukharan children. On Rabbi Chodaitov's arrival in *Eretz Yisroel* a special reception was arranged for him at Bnei Brak by Jews, now in Israel, whom he had helped to save during the Second World War.

Bukharan students at study and leisure.

learning *Torah* and *Chassidus*. These new immigrants soon adapted themselves to the *yeshivah*'s educational framework. Plans are already being implemented to erect additional buildings nearby to cater for the large demand for places at this *yeshivah*.

Chabad sees in this educational centre an important and essential stage in the absorption of the Bukharan community in *Eretz Yisroel* and a continuation of the work commenced by *Chabad Chassidim* among the Bukharan Jews in the Russian Diaspora over a century ago.

Another aspect of the *yeshivah* is the effect it has had on the older immigrants from Bukhara. Witnessing how the *yeshivah* has transformed the younger members of their community—who had previously only been able to learn some *Torah* in underground *chadorim* in their native land—into serious *yeshivah* students, these veterans are satisfied and appreciative that the spiritual future of their community is being well cared for.

The concern for the proper absorption and integration of the Bukharan community is one small but important link in the chain of *Chabad* endeavours in *Eretz Yisroel*. It is interesting to contrast it with the work being done at Chabad House in Jerusalem, a brief outline of which may be found earlier in this volume, the work among Russian academics being carried on by *Chabadnik* Professor Herman Branover, the famous physicist, and others; and the absorption and resettlement work at the second *Chabad* village, Nachalat Har Chabad.[1]

They are all aspects of *Chabad's* central theme. To promote through a love of every Jew a love of *Hashem* and the fulfilment of His Commandments.

[1] See page 219.

The Link

"Just as it is necessary for Jews possessing material wealth to share it with their poorer brethren, so also is it necessary for those who are spiritually wealthy to share that wealth with those less fortunate." This is the message that Rabbi Menachem M. Schneerson, the Lubavitcher Rebbe שליט״א, constantly relays to his followers, the *Chabad Chassidim*.

From what do the *Chabad Chassidim* derive their spiritual wealth, their special impetus?

Chabad's distinct philosophy was first set out as a way of life by the *Alter Rebbe*, Rabbi Shneur Zalman of Ladi, teaching that a *Chassid* must train himself for a life of faith and *avodah*, which will carry him to the highest level of *Chabad*: *chochmoh*, *binoh* and *daas*, forming a bond between Heaven and earth. His successors, the following generations of

Lubavitcher Rebbes, expounded on the *Alter Rebbe*'s basic and concise themes in talks, discourses and in countless volumes which have become classics of *Chassidic* literature and which are studied avidly, at different levels, by all *Chabad Chassidim* in addition to the normal learning done by all observant Jews.

But ask any *Chabad Chassid* from where he gains his spiritual strength and the most likely answer will be: "From the Rebbe, *er zoll gezundt zein.*"

From the inception of the *Chassidic* movement in Eastern Europe *Chassidim* visited their Rebbe whenever possible. Often covering long distances by primitive transport and under the most difficult conditions, they went to hear at first-hand the concepts that were bringing to the masses of Jews a revitalisation of faith and new hope where previously

gloom and despair had reigned. Strengthened by these visits they returned to their villages and towns to spread what they had heard and seen.

Modern means of travel have shortened distances and enabled more *Chassidim* to visit the Rebbe and participate in the *farbrengens* which the Rebbe holds to mark the special occasions in *Chabad* history which have become festivals in its calendar. On these visits the *Chassidim* are sometimes granted *yechidus* at which they discuss personal matters and, primarily, particular aspects of their work within the general scheme of *Chabad* activities. In this way there is a constant interchange of ideas, wider orbits are planned, new schemes formulated—but most of all there is a resurgence of energy, a new impetus, the re-igniting of a burning enthusiasm —an enthusiasm that will be infectious to others on the *Chassid*'s return.

Lod Airport and aboard the plane.

At "770"—770 Eastern Parkway, Brooklyn, New York—the building which houses the Rebbe's court, the power house of *Chabad* and the hub of the Lubavitch Empire, one can meet the complete spectrum of world Jewry. *Chassid*, *Torah* scholar, communal leader, professor, student, working-man, intellectual, head of State, they all see in the Rebbe the kaleidoscope of Jewish history, the personification of those great qualities of Jewish leadership with which the Jewish people have been graciously endowed throughout the centuries. One who, with an intense humility and profound understanding, relates to each individual in accordance with his individual spirit.

On a visit to New York, President Shazar in earnest conversation with the Lubavitcher Rebbe שליט״א and (opposite) on the way to the Reading of the *Megillah* at "770".

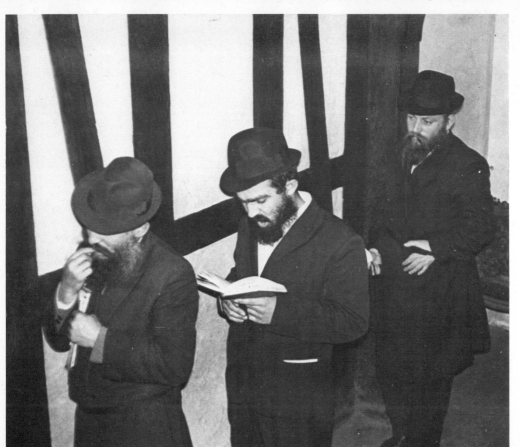

Left: Awaiting
yechidus; Chassidim
in prayer outside th
Rebbe's room.

Below: Amongst th
many important
visitors from all ove
the world awaiting
audience with the
Lubavitcher Rebbe
שליט״א is Mr.
Shimon Peres
(centre), Israeli
Cabinet Minister.

Left and centre left:
Chassidim on return
from a visit to the
Lubavitcher Rebbe
שליט״א bring
greetings to
President Shazar.

Centre right: General
"Arik" Sharon of
Israel Defence
Forces brings
greetings from the
Lubavitcher Rebbe
שליט״א to the
residents of Kfar
Chabad.

Left: President
Shazar receives
visitors recently
returned from the
Rebbe שליט״א

A *farbrengen* cannot easily be described or explained; it must be felt. Its effect on the *Chassidim* must be seen and experienced. It is at the *farbrengen* that the *Chassid* drinks from the waters of *Chassidic* wisdom, not the wisdom to be found merely by reading books, for it is at the *farbrengen* that the books come to life.

Those attending the Rebbe's *farbrengens* come away amazed at the sheer quantity and quality of erudition that the Rebbe pours forth hour after hour without recourse to notes. *Sichos* on a variety of subjects ranging from *nigleh* and *nistar* to current world affairs are punctuated by spirited singing and the whispered *"lechayim"* as each of the thousands

present seeks to catch the Rebbe's eye for a response to his toast.

Yud Shevat 5730 saw an innovation. The Rebbe's *farbrengen* was "broadcast" live for some six hours to Israel and was heard by *Chassidim* and others there. Since then, all succeeding major *farbrengens* which do not fall on *Shabbos* or *Yom Tov* have been similarly broadcast live to Israel, Australia, Great Britain, France, Italy and Belgium in addition to many cities in the United States and Canada.

In this way more and more *Chassidim* are able to participate directly in occasions which mean much to them and to increase the spiritual wealth which the Rebbe insists must be shared with others.

The Lubavitcher Rebbe's talks on special occasions are relayed to *Chassidim* throughout the world. These talks often lasting six or more hours link the world-wide Lubavitch Empire in one giant *farbrengen*, a source of great inspiration and impetus.

Telephone central control linking "770" to the rest of the world.

Kfar Chabad—the Rebbe's *farbrengen* in New York being relayed throughout the *Kfar* and recorded for further study.

The young and old listen to the Rebbe's discourses.

Translation of an article which appeared in "Maariv", the Israeli national evening newspaper, in 1964

"Salvation cannot come from those who follow the beaten track"
"The Torah given on Sinai needs a commander no less than the Sinai campaign"

EXCLUSIVE INTERVIEW WITH RABBI MENACHEM MENDEL SCHNEERSON—THE LUBAVITCHER REBBE. *by Geula Cohen*

I have been in the company of wise men, men of great learning and intelligence, men who were superior artists. But sitting opposite a true believer is quite a different matter. After having met a wise man you remain the same as before, you have become neither less of a fool nor more of a sage. The education of the man of learning hardly rubs off on you, nor does the artist endow you with any of his talents or inspiration. Not so with a believer. After having met him you are no longer the same. Though you may not have accepted his faith, you have nevertheless been embraced by it; for the true believer has faith in you as well.

The Lubavitcher Rebbe, Rabbi Menachem Mendel Schneerson, of Brooklyn, the spiritual leader of the World *Chabad* Movement, is both wise and learned, but above all he is a man of faith. And if faith be the art of truth, he is also an artist whose creation is the army of believers that he commands, the army of the Jewish faith, of the G–d of Israel and the People of Israel.

What about the belief in the Land of Israel?

To ask the Rebbe this question I first had to get to him. Jewish legend says nothing about how exactly the angels were received in audience by the L-rd, but had it wanted to it might well have taken its inspiration from the manner in which I managed to be received by the Lubavitcher Rebbe.

First of all, as with every ordinary mortal, there is, of course, the secretary with fixed reception hours and a long waiting list, except that here the secretary does not ask you what you intend to ask his boss. That is a matter between you and the Rebbe himself. Here, even if you may sometimes have to wait for days on end, anybody and everybody is eventually admitted. And the reception hours are not in daytime, but at night—all the night through. The day is for learning, the night for talking.

"At 11 o'clock at night?" I repeated, when told by Rabbi Hodakov, the Lubavitcher Rebbe's secretary, that this was the time of my appointment, for I was sure I had not heard right.

"Tomorrow, at 11 p.m.," came the laconic reply over the line connecting me with the Rebbe's court in Brooklyn.

"And why not in daytime?" When I asked this question, one of the Rebbe's followers looked at me as if I had come from the moon.

"During the day the Rebbe studies," came the answer, in a tone that left no room for further questions.

And indeed I found myself wondering whether this was not as it should be; whether at night the Heavens and the hearts of men might not be more open, more disposed to listen; at night when the barriers are down and man is closer to the truth. . . .

Perhaps the very fact that my thoughts were turning this way was already due to the incipient effect of the secret drug that begins to work on you, whether you want it or not, long before you actually meet the Rebbe; possibly from the moment that you decide you want to see him. However rationalistic you may be, all your sceptical questions begin to blush with shame. . . .

Consequently, I duly turned up at 11 p.m.; not alone, of course, because no woman can walk unaccompanied through the streets of Brooklyn at night. Here the terrors of the night assume special proportions, not only because of the stories you may have heard or read about a man or woman being killed at this or the other corner. People are being killed in other parts of the world as well, and not only at night but in daytime, too. Perhaps the peculiar terror of the Brooklyn nights is due to the fact that here nobody knows why a person is being killed; not only the killer but often also the victim is shrouded in obscure anonymity. You do not know whether you are being killed because you are a Jew, or in spite of your being a Jew; whether you have killed because you are a Negro or in spite of being a Negro; and whether you did so because you wanted to live or to die. Nothing is certain, except fear. In this Brooklyn night-time terror I now had to meet the Rebbe, but lest I met up with someone else before, I preferred to be properly escorted.

THE REBBE'S COURT

I don't remember a single preface in any book I have read that I did not skip. But from the long preliminaries I had to go through until I actually met the Rebbe, I learned that there are some preambles one cannot do without for the simple reason that they already constitute the beginning of the story. What the Rebbe has to say may be important, but still more important, perhaps also for the Rebbe himself and the *Chassidic* lore of the *Chabad* school, is to whom, when and where he said what he did. The atmosphere around him is no less relevant than what he actually says. The "how" may matter no less and perhaps even more than the "what". The Rebbe starts off where his court begins. His parlour begins at the porch. His followers are no less part of his personality than, as the *Chassidim* believe, all human beings form part of G–d. My interview therefore began the moment I entered the Rebbe's court and met his disciples.

The young men who crowded the premises, learning *Gemorrah*, can hardly be referred to as students or disciples. Although they were sitting in front of an open book they did not look like people learning something they did not know before. They seemed more like people in a laboratory who are experimenting with the spirit and its manifestations just as others experiment with matter: combining and decomposing, designing and synthesising. And all this is accompanied by their melodious humming. Much has been written about the *Chassidic* melodies, and much more will still be written about them. For they are tunes which have no end and no beginning. They seem to perpetuate the song which you sing so that someone else may continue it after you. Hearing that tune, it occurred to me that the Decalogue, the foundation of mankind, could never have been written and spoken according to a *Chassidic* melody. But it also occurred to me that mankind may not have been able to comply with this severe code had it not been for this softening melody. . . .

Those who were not leaning over their books were standing about and talking among themselves. Perhaps they were talking about everyday things, but the expression on their faces was enough to indicate that they were like frontline soldiers exchanging a few whispered words before going into action. The commander might have been invisible, but his presence made itself felt through and through. No orders were being given, but they might be at any moment; and everybody was ready to listen and obey.

THE REBBE'S "PEACE CORPS"

I, too, was waiting for my orders to go in to the Rebbe. The time was a quarter past eleven, half past eleven . . . when will it be my turn to be called in? I was just about to ask one of the young men in the court office when a well-dressed young woman came in, with a patter of high heels, her blonde hair streaming out beneath her kerchief. Before I could see her face I could hear her half-choking voice: "Have you got an answer yet?" Instead of answering her the young man she had addressed went over to a pile of letters, pulled out the one she had written, and told her that the Rebbe's answer was right in there. The woman snatched it away, opened it and read it on the spot. For a moment her eyes froze over. There might have been tears as well—of joy or of sorrow, who can tell? Leaving without a goodbye she was back again as soon as she had gone.

"I have another question. May I ask the Rebbe another question?"

"Of course," she is told. "At any time and about anything you may wish."

Her face lights up with happiness.

"Poor woman," says the man to me after she has left. "All her life she's been going to psychiatrists, and they didn't help her at all. How could they help her if all they have is knowledge and no faith? They don't love her; they love only their books. How can one help without love?" I became curious about this young man.

He was about twenty-five, and it transpired that he had only recently returned from a trip to Australia undertaken on the Rebbe's behalf. "What am I doing here—what do you mean? I have a wife and a family but one day the Rebbe told me to go on a trip and I asked no questions about where and why. Nobody questions the Rebbe. His every word is an order. He doesn't say things that might have remained unsaid or could have been said otherwise. So I took my family and went. What did I do in Australia? Whatever I was told. There are people being sent round the world to distribute food and money among the Jews, but what the Jews really need is spiritual food—a bit of love, of *Yiddishkeit*. The Rebbe's orders were for me to go and give them love, to encourage them, to bring a little Jewishness into their souls. There is social assistance and there is First Aid for physical ailments, but we are concerned with First Aid for spiritual ills. Of course we are concerned with people's physical wellbeing, too. Have you heard about the 'Maccabees' who organised the defence of the Brooklyn Jews during the riots? The man who organised them, Rabbi Shraga, is one of ours. . . . It was a great honour for me to have been sent on a mission by the Rebbe but I am only one of many hundreds and thousands. We have a whole army here, our Peace Corps. This is our headquarters. From here the Rebbe despatches his soldiers to the various fronts. Wherever there is a single Jew there is a front for us to fight on, with the Holy Scriptures in our hands and the love of Israel in our hearts. These are our weapons. If there is some Jewish corner in the world that is inaccessible by car, we go there on donkeys. There is nothing that can stop us. All we have in mind is that the Rebbe's orders should be carried out to the full, that we should be able to come back and report to him: 'Mission accomplished.'"

But the Peace Corps, as I am informed by the office manager, is only one of the many ramifications of the Lubavitcher Court.

THE SUN NEVER SETS OVER THE LUBAVITCH EMPIRE

"People used to say that the sun never sets over the British Empire, but it is already going down. Not so with the Lubavitch Empire. We are growing stronger from day to day," he said. "Have you heard about our publishing house? It is the biggest publisher of Jewish writings in the world, issuing books in over ten languages. We also have hundreds of *yeshivos* with some 30,000 students. Do you know our village in Israel? There'll be many more such communities. Once a week we publish an information bulletin, circulated by the ITA News Agency.

"Who are the people who come to see the Rebbe? Well, who doesn't? *Chassidim* and *Misnagdim*, men and women, tradesmen and scholars, young and old, Jews and Gentiles, leaders and statesmen; including the present President of Israel—did you know he was one of ours? As for his correspondence—again, with whom doesn't he correspond? Even with Ben Gurion. What about? That is the Rebbe's own affair. Nobody opens the letters that are addressed to him. He himself opens them all, and answers them, too.

"What do Jews ask about as a rule? About matters of religion and how to make a living; about their personal affairs and about politics. In short—about everything. There is no question he cannot answer. Where there is faith, one is able to answer every question. For him there are no important and unimportant questions. Every question calls for a true answer. . . . Excuse me a minute."

I hadn't heard the bell ringing, but the secretary jumped over to the phone and immediately left the room. Unwittingly I found myself adjusting the kerchief I had tied over my head in anticipation of my interview with the Rebbe. I was just in time, for the next moment the secretary was back to tell me, with the air of one presenting a most marvellous gift: "That's it now; come along with me."

He may have said some more, but I no longer heard him because I was too busy covering up for my sudden palpitations, telling myself not to be a fool, that there was no need to get excited, that this wasn't my first midnight appointment. . . .

MIDNIGHT APPOINTMENT

When the door closed behind me and I remained alone with the Rebbe the time was twelve midnight, but the Rebbe rose from behind his desk to receive me with a smile that spelled noon rather than midnight.

If that is what you are interested in, you may see a handsome face with a kind and gracious expression, a black hat above and a grey beard below. Alternatively you may see nothing but a pair of eyes fixed upon you not in order to see but in order to discover and reveal. Then it won't be so pleasant for you if you have something to hide, if your intention was to deceive. You try to button yourself up anew, because you feel some of your buttons may have suddenly burst. Is it because the Rebbe really has magic eyes or is it because you have brought the magic along with you as a result of your night-time experience and the purge administered by the Rebbe's disciples? However, the question of cause and effect no longer matters. What matters is to try and remember why one has come in the first place. And so I start by introducing myself.

Except that it isn't necessary. He knows more about me than I might be able to tell him. He knows not only what I have done but what I ought to have done, not only what I am doing now but what I am not doing and should do. His disciples had told me that he reads the papers every day and took a lively interest in Israel, but it was a little frightening nevertheless.

"I understand that you are writing for the press now. Well, that's all right, but it isn't the main thing. The young generation, that is the main thing. One has to talk to youngsters, not write for them. Why aren't you talking to them? Why is nobody talking to them? They are waiting for someone to talk with but nobody does. They are being addressed in lofty speeches, but nobody talks to them, and then people are surprised that they remain indifferent."

The Rebbe does not speak with me in Yiddish but in Hebrew. His accent may not be the purest Sephardi, but his language is the language of the Bible. And however exciting his words, his voice remains level and calm.

"What youth is waiting for is an order which must be given in the same voice and tone in which all the great commands were issued to the People of Israel. They may obey or they may not, but that is what they are waiting for. But there is no commander to issue that order. Where are they all? No salvation can come from those who walk in the beaten path, but only from those who break new ground. What has happened to all those who were once burning with the holy fire of a holy war that they are now dealing with such bagatelles as whether people should pay a little more or a little less income tax instead of thinking about the urgent concerns of the Jewish people as a whole? Where are those who at one time knew how to issue commands? I believe physics: that energy can never disappear. Forces that have once existed will exist for ever. Therefore I believe in the everlasting force of the Jewish people. Whatever forces there may once have been in its youth still exist and need only be evoked. Once there were those who knew how to evoke them —where have they gone?

סיפורים מפורשים בתנ״ך ולקחיהם

"Everybody is in a rut, following a course of dull mediocrity. And, as you know, there is nothing worse than conformity. To be carried away by the current is very much like dying. Creativity begins by swimming against the current. What is needed is someone to start swimming against the current. I am not preaching, G–d forbid, revolt, only protest against the set pattern of conformity. If the present set-up has turned into a prison, one must find ways to break away from it. That does not mean breaking the law, but fighting against the law. Yet everybody, the entire Jewish nation, is conforming to the set pattern, and there is no one to lead the way out. . . ."

The Rebbe's voice is filled with deep despair, but without pathos. "Have you ever calculated how many precious youth-hours are going to waste every day? The use of every such hour could wreak wonders. Instead of giving orders the leaders make speeches and the young people go to cafés and waste their precious irretrievable time. Do you remember them during the Sinai campaign, how they rose like one man because there was a commander whose orders were such as they had been waiting for, even if they did not know it beforehand? Just give them an order as was done during the Sinai campaign—never mind the particulars, all that matters is that it should ignite some spark as it did then—and you will see how all the latent forces will rise up again. . . .

"It would hardly matter if everything were as it should be in the Land of Israel and in the Diaspora. But it isn't. All the 'ideals' and all the 'panaceas' have failed and only very, very little has so far been accomplished. Never in the 3,500-year history of the Jewish nation was there a period without any prospects; sometimes the chances were used and at other times they were allowed to escape. But never in the whole history of the Jewish people has there been a period which offered as many opportunities as the present, and never has there been a period when so few were utilised."

THE TORAH ALSO NEEDS A COMMANDER

Until I suddenly heard the sharp ringing of a bell I had not realised the vast silence that dwelt in this room. The ringing came from outside; from the office, presumably. I gathered that my time had run out. But it did not occur to me to get up, and I went on sitting there as if there had been no ringing. Despite the repeated exhortation of the bell, the sound of the Rebbe's voice assured me that this was not yet the end.

"Every day that goes by is a tremendous loss. What it takes ten years to do in the Diaspora can be done in ten days in the Land of Israel, provided one gets down to the latent spark. A fire can go out, but a spark never. Our youth is asleep without knowing it, and those who address it with speeches are surprised at their not hearing. Unless they hear their own words, they are not aroused.

"What exactly are the words of our youth? I cannot tell. The words will follow with the inner force of the imperative. They must come from deep inside. The main thing is the awakening, the pioneering spirit. Once the vanguard is there, the banner may follow. Now there are many banners, but what are they all worth without anybody to walk ahead of them and carry them? Take those boys in Israel who throw stones on people who desecrate the Sabbath—I believe they have the spirit, there is something they really care about. I am not suggesting that they should throw stones on the Sabbath, G—d forbid, but I feel that they care, that there is something burning inside them, and that is the main thing. Then I can try to convince them that they are using the wrong means, to divert their fire into the right channels. . . .

"On the other hand the young people who are coming from the Land of Israel to study at foreign universities—they are not pioneers. What can they learn abroad that they cannot learn in the Holy Land? If a man leaves his home to go to the North Pole or climb a mountain at the risk of his life to satisfy his thirst for knowledge one may call him a pioneer. A young man who goes from Brooklyn to the Negev and risks his life on the border may be called a pioneer. But leaving Israel to study at a university in Brooklyn—that is mere hankering after comfort, not pioneering.

"Take our *yeshivah* students—they study, too. But in order to teach they go everywhere in the world where there are Jews, not to sit there in a *yeshivah* but to open new academies. They knock on every door. They find their way to non-religious *kibbutzim* in Israel and to assimilated homes in the Diaspora. The spirit of Judaism is the one ideal that has not failed like all the rest. Only the values of religion persist unscathed and unaltered. So far nothing has been found to replace them. And that is precisely why no compromise is possible in this respect. Everything may be done to facilitate its teaching, but nothing to facilitate its observance. Attempts to compromise will only alienate our youth rather than bring it closer to our religion. Israel's youth wants no compromises. But here, too, no leader has been found, no commander who will issue the order, as in the Sinai campaign."

I SHALL COME WHEN THE MESSIAH ARRIVES

It is getting close to two o'clock. The bell has stopped ringing. It has probably given up. But ringing in my own ears was the redoubled sound of my question:

"Why won't you come and give the order?"

"My place is where my words are likely to be obeyed. Here I am being listened to, but in the Land of Israel I won't be heard. There, our youth will follow only somebody who has sprung up from its own ranks and speaks its own language. The Messiah will be a man of flesh and blood, visible and tangible, a man whom others may follow. And he will come."

"He has been on his way for quite a while," I found myself saying.

"But he is very near and we must be prepared for him at any moment, because he may have come just one moment before."

סיפורים מפורשים בתנ״ך ולקחיהם

(The surrounding Hebrew text in the three columns is dense and partially cut off at the page margins.)

זכותו של יהודי לחו״ד בארץ ישראל

לשאלת הנשים הנכריות — מימי עזרא הסופר ועד עתה

יהודי התפוצות

The Lamplighters

Chanukah at the Suez Canal—a *Chabadnik* visits soldiers at the front.

"What is a *Chassid?*" someone once asked Rabbi Sholom Dovber. The fifth Lubavitcher Rebbe replied: "A *Chassid* is a street-lamplighter."

In those days there used to be a man whose job it was to light the street-lamps by means of a torch carried at the end of a long pole.

The lamps were there in readiness but they needed to be lit. Sometimes lamps are not as easily accessible as those on street corners, but there must be someone to light even those lamps so that their potential is not wasted—so that they may illuminate the path of others.

Chassidic philosophy compares man's soul to a flame. King Solomon

Right: Rachel's tomb.
Below: At Central Bus Station.

writes: "The soul of a man is the lamp of G–d." It is also written: "A *mitzvah* is a candle and the *Torah* is the light."

Street-lamplighters are an anachronism, but the parallel remains. Throughout the world today there are Jews, young and old, who, in the modern idiom, are waiting to be "turned-on".

Throughout the world, wherever there are Jews, one will find Lubavitch or encounter the influence of *Chabad*. In Israel, quite naturally, one finds *Chabad Chassidim* everywhere. *Chabad Chassidim* who put their personal affairs aside in order to light up the souls of their fellow-Jews with the light of *Torah* and *mitzvos*; souls that are waiting to be "turned-on".

Sometimes they are just around the corner, at a bus-stop in Tel Aviv,

The truck . . .

. . . the helicopter

. and the tank.

or at The Wall in Jerusalem; sometimes on the heights of Golan, in the desert of Sinai or at the Canal at Suez.

Sometimes the "lighting" is accomplished through an experience, by a word or a friendly action. Sometimes, but rarely, it is rapid; often the spark is hardly discernible; usually it is a slow process. Success is hard to measure and anyway it is not the criterion, for whatever the reason, whichever the method, the important thing is that there must be those who are prepared to "do".

This is the mission of the *Chabad Chassid*, the modern lamplighter, who uses together with the latest means of communication—the aeroplane, the helicopter, the tank, the truck, the tape recorder and the radio—the never-old means of "turning-on": the friendly smile, the sympathetic heart, the cheering word, the kindly action, the welcoming hand, the *moshol*, the *nigun* and the dance.

habadniks visit soldiers at different theatres of war.

. . . the friendly smile

. . . the sympathetic heart

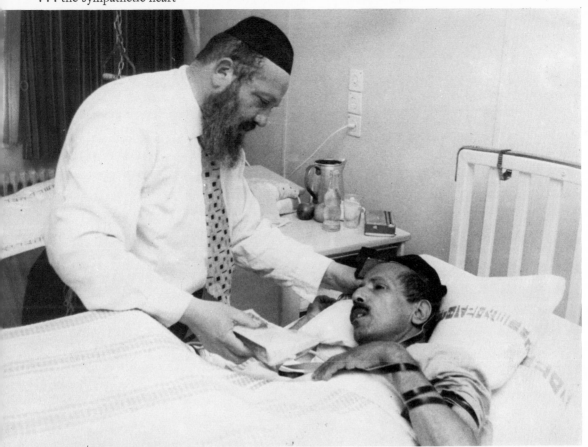

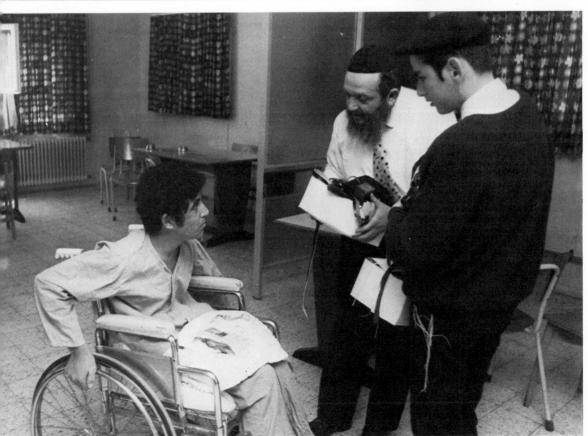

. . . the cheering word.

. . . the kindly action

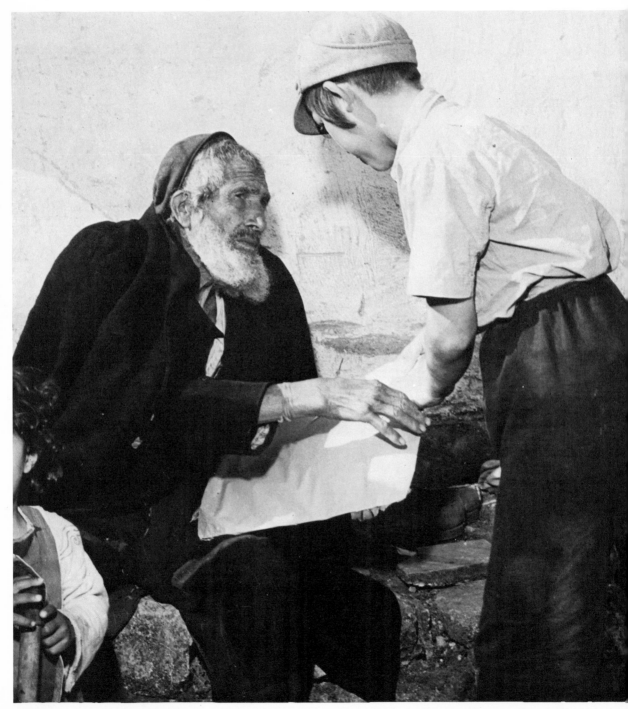

. . . the welcoming hand

. . . the *moshol*

. the *nigun*

. . . and the dance.

1972

A birthday celebration

This book, like the work of *Chabad* in *Eretz Yisroel* and throughout the world, really has no end. But it must halt somewhere, so how better than the way it began . . . at a birthday celebration.

The date was 11th *Nissan* 5732 (1972). The occasion: the seventieth birthday of the leader of the world-wide Lubavitch-*Chabad* movement, Rabbi Menachem M. Schneerson, the Lubavitcher Rebbe שליט״א.

The planes landed at Kennedy International Airport and the taxis pulled up in front of the Lubavitch headquarters in New York. Thousands of *Chassidim* from all over the world were gathering to participate in the celebration of this important and happy occasion. They came from all the corners of the earth: Israel, Morocco, Italy, France, Australia, Great Britain, Scandinavia and the Americas. Friends who had not met for years crushed excitedly into the small entrance hall. They had at least one thing in common—a dedication to the future of Judaism. Many were, in their own right, leaders in their communities, but today they gathered as disciples of their great leader. For, to his tens of thousands of *Chassidim* and to hundreds of thousands of supporters and admirers around the world he is "the Rebbe"; the most dominant figure in world-Jewry.

But this was not just a parochial occasion. Heads of State, Statesmen and other world leaders, aware of the special contribution made by the Rebbe and *Chabad* in so many fields, particularly in education and with youth, were eager to add their congratulations in letters and telegrams.

There was an air of expectancy as the thousands of *Chassidim* made their way to the large *shul* where the Rebbe would address the gathering.

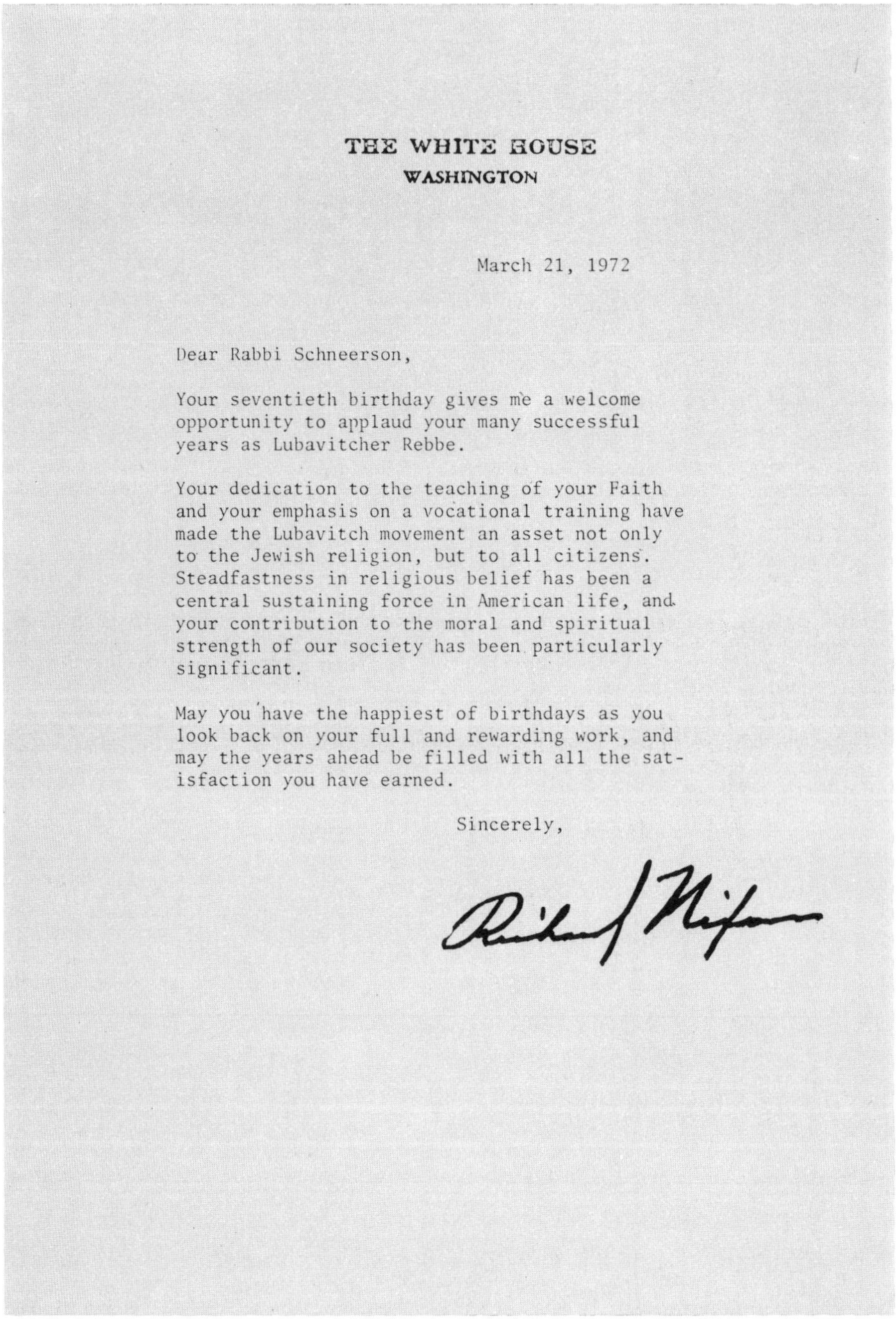

THE WHITE HOUSE
WASHINGTON

March 21, 1972

Dear Rabbi Schneerson,

Your seventieth birthday gives me a welcome opportunity to applaud your many successful years as Lubavitcher Rebbe.

Your dedication to the teaching of your Faith and your emphasis on a vocational training have made the Lubavitch movement an asset not only to the Jewish religion, but to all citizens. Steadfastness in religious belief has been a central sustaining force in American life, and your contribution to the moral and spiritual strength of our society has been particularly significant.

May you have the happiest of birthdays as you look back on your full and rewarding work, and may the years ahead be filled with all the satisfaction you have earned.

Sincerely,

Richard Nixon

Letter from President Nixon.

Mr. Herman Wouk (extreme right) showing letter sent by
President Nixon to the Lubavitcher Rebbe שליט״א on the
occasion of the Rebbe's 70th birthday. The letter, one of
many received from Heads of States and leading figures
throughout the world, is reproduced opposite.

Above: Israel's Ambassador to the U.S.A., General Yitzchok Rabin, a "770" to bring 70 birthday greetings to the Rebbe א״טיש from the State of Israel.

Left: Ambassador Rabin joins *Chassidim* in dance at birthday celebrations.

It is not easy to paint the scene. Of those present, some found seats at the tables leading from the head table at which the Rebbe would sit; the majority standing on tiers of tables and benches lined the walls almost to the ceiling. In some dozen countries throughout the world tens of thousands who were not able to journey to New York listened to the "live" relay of the proceedings.

A section of the huge gathering which assembled at "770" to be with the Rebbe שליט"א on his 70th birthday.

The first verse of the 71st Psalm, the whole of which the Rebbe and his *Chassidim* would recite each day throughout the coming year in accordance with *Chassidic* tradition, had been put to music. (*"B'Cho Hashem Choseesee, Ahl Ayvosho L'olam"*—"In You, my G–d I have put my trust, I shall never be shamed.")

The singing started and gained momentum. The gathering was unified in happiness and purpose.

As the Rebbe walked into the vast *shul* which surely could not contain another person, the crowd parted and a path opened. A hush fell. The Rebbe sat down at the centre of a white-decked table at the head of the room, framed by the leaders of Lubavitch *Chassidim* and great Rabbinical authorities seated behind him. His cup was filled with wine. The Rebbe recited the *berocho*, drank the wine and raised his cup: *"Lechayim"*—"To life."

The pitch of excitement grew.

The Rebbe began to speak in *Yiddish* and Hebrew:[1]

"Many of my acquaintances have suggested that now, upon reaching my seventieth birthday, it would be the appropriate time to think about relaxing the immense work load resting on my shoulders and begin planning for eventual retirement."

He turned to those seated nearest him and told them to sing a lively *nigun*, for what he intended to say next would require the spirit of melody. The voices rose, the tempo built and the swaying grew. The Rebbe motioned with his hands, faster, faster. The gathering was welded into one abounding and kinetic force.

With one swift motion of the Rebbe's hand the singing stopped.

"To which I reply," the Rebbe continued, "a man's years cannot and

[1] The following is a free translation of excerpts from the Lubavitcher Rebbe's address at his seventieth birthday celebration.

should not be determined by his birth certificate or passport but rather by his feelings and attitudes towards life and, more important, by his accomplishments and attainments during his past years. Furthermore, we have the words of our great Psalmist: 'Our days thereon be seventy years and, with strength, eighty years'; all that was lacking in man's first seventy years can be fulfilled and complemented with renewed vigour and 'strength' in the coming years.

"It is well known that man is not satisfied with what he possesses. He who has one hundred shekels wants two hundred. Within the framework of Judaism this desire in man can be used to enlarge and broaden the intensity of one's involvement and commitment in matters of *Torah* and its Commandments. In our situation here, what is desired is an increase of *Torah* institutions.

"This coming year we will be entering my seventy-first year. My desire, therefore, is that during this seventy-first year seventy-one new institutions be established for the furtherance of Jewish commitment and observance. This request is extended to all those who will hearken to my words and will act as my agents, as my hands and feet."

A spontaneous gasp escaped from the gathering. Everyone present believed that they were working to full capacity; that all possible resources were already mobilised.

As if reading their minds, the Rebbe continued: "There are those who will be frightened by this monumental task and ask: 'From where will the resources come for all these new projects?' Ten per cent of all expenses incurred in establishing all these institutions will be covered by the monies of Fund Seventy.[1]

"There will be little bureaucracy and red tape involved in receiving the funds. I promise that with dedication and perseverance these institutions will be established and in turn they can be an added impetus to increase the amount to twice seventy-one and four times seventy-one until 'the world will be filled with the knowledge of G–d like the waters which cover the seas.'"

Once the Rebbe's words had sunk in, a new vision opened in the hearts and minds of those gathered. The Rebbe had requested these new institutions. Without a doubt it could be done. The challenge must be met.

B'Cho Hashem Choseesee.

Over a year has passed since that memorable birthday celebration and, of course, the target was reached and exceeded in that wonderful year of achievement.

In Israel alone *Chabad* inaugurated more than seventy-one new projects, small and large, in that year.

[1] Fund Seventy was established with special donations and contributions offered to the Rebbe in honour of his seventieth birthday. The fund was disbursed towards the cost of the new institutions established in the Rebbe's seventy-first year.

But the work continues, the story has no end until, as the Rebbe שליט״א said: "The world will be filled with the knowledge of G-d like the waters which cover the seas."

Glossary

Adamah. Ground; dust.

Adar. Hebrew month in the Jewish year; occurs late winter or beginning of spring.

Agadeta (popular expression for **Aggadah**). lit. Narration. Whereas the *Halachah* deals with Jewish law and ordinances, all other matters such as prayers, philosophy, theology, ethics, history, etc. are classified as *Aggadah*.

Ahavas Yisroel. Love of fellow Jew.

Aliyah. lit. Going up. Term used in connection with being called up to the reading of the *Torah* in the synagogue. Also used in connection with immigration to Israel.

Alter Rebbe. lit. Old Rabbi. Among *Chabad Chassidim*, the term *Alter Rebbe* refers to Rabbi Shneur Zalman of Ladi. Was first used during the time of Rabbi Menachem Mendel of Lubavitch (third generation), to differentiate between the incumbent Rebbe (always known as "the Rebbe"), the previous Rebbe ("the *Mittler Rebbe*") and the first Rebbe ("the *Alter Rebbe*").

Amidah. lit. Standing. The prayer of the Eighteen Benedictions, recited standing.

Anash. Acrostic of *Anshei shlomeinu*.

Anshei shlomeinu. lit. Men of our peace. Fraternity. A term used to denote particular groups in general, and especially in frequent use among *Chassidim* when referring to their own group(s). The term is of Biblical origin. (Jer. 38:22; Obadiah 1:7; Gen. 34:21.)

Ari Z.L. See Luria, Isaac. Z.L. abbreviation for *Zichrona Levrocho*—of Blessed memory.

Aron Hakodesh. Holy Ark, in the centre of the east wall of the synagogue, which houses the Scrolls of the *Torah*.

Ashkenazi (pl. **Ashkenazim**). Term originally applied to Jews of Germany and northern France, as distinct from Jews living in the Spanish and Mediterranean countries, called *Sephardim*.

Later, the Jews of Poland, Russia and the Scandinavian countries were also called *Ashkenazim*.

Ato horaiso lodaas. To you it was shown that you might know.

Av. Hebrew month in the late summer.

Av Beth Din. Head of the *Beth Din*.

Avodah. Service. Refers to the service and worship of G-d.

Avodah shebalev. Divine service of the heart, i.e. prayer.

Baal Korah (properly **Baal Keriah**). lit. Master of reading. Term used for the official reader of the specific portion of the *Torah* read before the congregation in the synagogue on *Shabbosos* and *Yomim Tovim*.

Baal teshuvah (pl. **baalei teshuvah**). A penitent; penitents. See *teshuvah*.

Baalei battim. lit. House owners. Members of the community.

Barmitzvah. lit. Son of the command. The ceremony marking a boy's thirteenth birthday, when he attains adulthood in Jewish life and becomes religiously responsible for his own conduct.

B'Cho Hashem Choseesee. In you, my G-d I have put my trust. (Psalm 71:1.)

B'Cho Hashem Choseesee, Ahl Ayvosho L'olam. In you, my G-d I have put my trust, I shall never be shamed. (Psalm 71:1.)

Beis Hamedrash (pl. **Batei Medrashim**). lit. House(s) of study. Place(s) of prayer and learning.

Beis Hamikdosh. The Holy Temple in ancient Jerusalem. The first one was built by King Solomon and destroyed by Nebuchadnezzar of Babylon. The second was built by the returning exiles from Babylon and destroyed by Titus of Rome (70 C.E.).

Bentsch; bentsching (Yiddish). To say Grace after a meal. To bless. To pronounce a blessing (e.g. over a *lulav* and *esrog*).

Berocho (pl. **Berochos**). Blessing(s). Benediction(s).

Beth Din. lit. House of Law. Rabbinical court.

Bikur Cholim. Visiting the sick. Applied to the *mitzvah* of a Jewish person visiting the sick and comforting them during their illness. Some Jewish congregations appoint committees specially for this purpose. The rabbis derived the importance of this *mitzvah* from G–d's visit to Abraham after his circumcision. (Gen. 18:1.)

Bimah. Elevated platform in the synagogue on which the desk stands for reading the *Sefer Torah* and *Prophets*.

Binoh. Understanding; comprehension; intellectual grasp. One of the three primary intellect powers. (See also *Chabad*.)

Bnei Avrohom Avinu. Sons of our father Abraham.

Boruch Habo. Blessed be your coming.

Boruch Hashem. Blessed be the L–rd.

Chabad. Acrostic of *Chochmoh* (wisdom), *Binoh* (understanding), *Daas* (knowledge). Branch of *Chassidic* movement founded by Rabbi Shneur Zalman, based on intellectual approach to the service of G–d.

Chabadnik(s). Follower(s) of the philosophy of *Chabad*.

Chadorim. See *cheder*.

Chanukah. Feast of Dedication; begins *Kislev* 25 and lasts for eight days.

Chassid (pl. **Chassidim**). Adherent(s) of the *Chassidic* movement; follower(s) of a *Chassidic* Rebbe.

Chassidic. Appertaining to *Chassidism* and *Chassidus*.

Chassidism. Movement founded by Rabbi Israel Baal Shem Tov.

Chassidus. Philosophy of *Chassidism*.

Chazan. Cantor. Synagogue official who leads the congregants in prayer.

Cheder (pl. **chadorim**). lit. Room(s). Now used to denote elementary religious school where the curriculum is exclusively religious, i.e. Bible, *Talmud*, etc. Formerly also used to denote any school of religious instruction. For example, the Maggid of Meseritch's *cheder* was for pupils who already knew the whole *Talmud* by heart.

Chevra Kadisha. lit. Holy Society. Voluntary organisation whose members engage in the *mitzvah* of attending to the ritual washing and burial of a dead person.

Chevra Linno. Society for providing people to stay (overnight if necessary) with sick people in their homes.

Chevras Gemillas Chasodim. Society for the *mitzvah* of performing acts of kindness. Charity in its broadest sense, e.g. giving charity, giving a loan to a needy person, visiting the sick, burying the dead, comforting those in mourning, etc.

Chinuch. Education.

Chochmoh. Wisdom; concept. One of the three primary intellect powers. (See also *Chabad*.)

Chol-Hamoed. Intermediate days of the festivals of *Pesach* and *Succos*.

Chumash (pl. **Chumashim**). Pentateuch; Five Books of Moses.

Daas. Knowledge; concentration; depth. One of the three primary intellect powers. (See also *Chabad*.)

Daven; davenned; davenning. To pray; prayed; praying.

Dayan Ho'Emes lit. The true Judge. The last words of the blessing recited on hearing bad tidings.

Derech. Way. Path.

Divrei Torah. Words of *Torah*.

Dvekus. Cleaving; attachment to G–d; devotion.

Elul. Last month of the Hebrew calendar. Period of repentance in preparation for *Rosh Hashonoh*.

Er zoll gezundt zein (Yiddish). He should be well.

Eretz Yisroel. Land of Israel.

Erev. Evening. Used to mean "day before", as, for example, *erev Shabbos*.

Esrog. The citron fruit used at *Succos*. One of the "Four Kinds".

Farbrengen(s) (Yiddish). Gathering of *Chassidim* to discuss *Chassidus*, recount tales of the Rebbes and *Chassidim*, and to give each other moral exhortation. In addition to its immediate purpose, a *farbrengen* serves to strengthen the bonds among *Chassidim*.

Gabbai (pl. **gabbayim**). Warden(s) of synagogue.

Gaon (pl. **Gaonim**). Excellency; title of honour for distinguished *Talmudist(s)*.

Gemorrah (pl. **Gemorros**). The work based on, and directly interpreting the *Mishna*. Together they constitute the *Talmud*.

Geulo. Redemption.

Gevir. A wealthy man.

Golus. Exile.

Hachnossas kalloh. lit. Introducing. Dowering the bride. A term applied to the *mitzvah* of assisting to provide poor girls with dowries, trousseaus, etc.

Hachnossas orchim. Entertaining wayfarers. A term applied to the *mitzvah* of hospitality.

Hadran. Conclusion lecture.

Haggadah. lit. The telling. Traditional text read on the first two nights of Passover. (*Seder* nights.)

Hagomel. Special blessing of thanks for deliverance from danger or illness or after an overseas journey or on being released from prison. This blessing is recited at the time of being called up to the Reading of the *Torah* in the synagogue.

Halachah. Jewish law.

Halachic. Appertaining to *Halachah*.

Hanholah. lit. Management. Administration.

Haphtorah. lit. Conclusion. Selection from the *Prophets* read immediately after the reading of the *Torah* on *Shabbosos*, *Yomim Tovim* and other occasions. One special blessing is recited before reading the *Haphtorah* and four special blessings are recited on its conclusion. The *Haphtorah* is generally related in some way to the portion of *Torah* or, if it is a special *Shabbos*, to the occasion. Often, the *Haphtorah* is read by a boy celebrating his *Barmitzvah*.

Hashem. lit. The Name. Alternative name for G–d.

Hayom laasoisom. Today is the day to do it.

Iyar. A month of the Hebrew calendar (following the month of *Nissan*).

Jerushalmi. Term applied to the native-born of Jerusalem.

Kabbalah. lit. Received tradition. Esoteric Jewish lore; mysticism; inner interpretation of the *Torah*.

Kabbalistic. Appertaining to *Kabbalah*.

Kabbolos Shabbos. lit. Acceptance of the *Shabbos*. Prayers said to usher in the Sabbath.

Kain yirboo. lit. Thus they shall increase.

Kapporos. Atonement. The custom, prior to *Yom Kippur*, of rotating a rooster (for men) or a hen (for women) over the head while praying that the fowl, when slaughtered, should serve as a substitute and atonement for the individual and his/her sins. One should not think that this act in itself is an atonement, but rather one should seek to awaken in oneself an awareness that one may deserve punishment because of one's transgressions and that one should exert all one's strength to repent and seek G–d's mercy.

Kashrus. *Torah* dietary observances.

Kfar. Village.

Kibbutz (pl. **kibbutzim**). Collective settlement(s).

Kibbutznik. A member of a *kibbutz*.

Kinos. Elegies.

Kislev. A month of the Hebrew calendar. (Third from *Tishrei*.)

Klal. Community.

Klal Yisroel. Community (whole people) of Israel.

Koheles. *Ecclesiastes.* The book *Koheles* is contained in the "Writings" (*Kesuvim*), the last section of the Bible. It is universally quoted because it contains numerous sayings of wisdom in reference to man's conduct, his relationship with other people and his manifold experiences in life.

Kohen (pl. **Kohanim**). Priest(s); descendants of Aaron.

Kolel. Academy of higher learning where married men learn and if necessary are supported financially.

Kosel. The Wall. An abbreviation for *Kosel Ma'arovi*.

Kosel Ma'arovi. Western Wall. The only remnant of the *Beis Hamikdosh*.

Kosher. lit. Fit. Food permitted by the Dietary Laws.

Lag B'Omer. Thirty-third day of the Omer. Occurs on *Iyar* 18. Traditionally observed as a reminder of the cessation of a plague which threatened to destroy the students of Rabbi Akiva. *Lag B'Omer* is also observed as the anniversary of the death of Rabbi Shimon ben Yochai.

Lechayim. lit. To life. Customary toast in Jewish circles.

Lecho Dodi. lit. Come my beloved. The opening words of one of the best-known hymns sung in the Friday *Kabbolos Shabbos* service. Written by Solomon (Shlomoh Ha Levi) Alkabetz in the middle of the sixteenth century. The initial letters of the first eight verses spell out the name of the author. Each verse of this hymn is followed by the refrain: "Come my beloved to meet the bride (Sabbath); let us welcome the presence of the Sabbath." It is customary for the congregation to turn towards the entrance of the synagogue while reciting the last verse.

Lehavdil. To distinguish or to separate.

Likutei Amarim. lit. "Collected Essays" otherwise the *Tanya*.

Lulav. Palm branch. One of the four species of plants used on *Succos*.

Luria, Isaac (1534–1572). Born in Jerusalem to German immigrant parents, his surname was Ashkenazi. After being orphaned in early childhood he went to Egypt where he was brought up and educated by his uncle. He lived there as a hermit for thirteen years engrossed in the study of the *Zohar*. In 1569 he went to Safed, then the centre of *Kabbalistic* study, where he settled. His pupils named him the *Ari* (Lion) *Ha Kodoysh*, an acrostic of "Ashkenazi Rabbi Isaac" with the attribute of "The Holy". His ideas and teachings, received by his pupils orally, were posthumously recorded by his pupil Rabbi Chaim Vital.

Maamar (pl. **maamorim**). lit. Word or article. In *Chabad* circles the term refers to a formal discourse by a *Chabad* Rebbe. The form is usually a quotation from Bible or *Talmud*, questions to be discussed, and the interpretation according to the doctrines of *Chabad*. *Maamorim* are delivered in *Yiddish* but published in Hebrew and/or *Yiddish*. They may be, occasionally, on the popular level.

Maariv. Evening prayers.

Machnes orach. One who performs the *mitzvah* of *hachnossas orchim*.

Machpelah. Doubled; two tiers. The Cave of Machpelah is situated in Hebron. It was originally purchased by Abraham as a burying place for his wife Sarah because Adam and Eve were already buried there. The Cave is the burying place of the Patriarchs, Abraham, Isaac and Jacob and the Matriarchs, Sarah, Rebecca and Leah.

Maftir. The concluding verses of the portion of the *Torah* read on *Shabbosos* and *Yomim Tovim*. After the required quorum are called to the Reading of the Law (minimum of seven on *Shabbos*, six on *Yom Kippur* and five on other Holy Days), a member of the congregation is called for *Maftir* and the concluding verses of the *Sidra* are repeated by the *Baal Korah*. In most synagogues the person so called also recites the *Haphtorah* and the blessings which precede and succeed it. Colloquially the term includes the *Haphtorah*.

Maggid. Preacher.

MaHaRaSh. The fourth Lubavitcher Rebbe, Rabbi Shmuel, is referred to by Lubavitch *Chassidim* as the *MaHaRaSh*.

Mashgiach (pl. **mashgichim**). Supervisor(s). In *yeshivah* the *mashgiach* supervises the *shiurim* and learning. In a *Chassidic yeshivah* the *mashgiach* supervises the learning of *nigleh*.

Person(s) appointed to supervise the observance of *kashrus* laws in the preparation of food.

Mashke. Drink; usually refers to alcoholic beverage.

Mashpiah (pl. **Mashpi'im**). Instructor(s) of *Chassidus*, especially responsible for influencing the spiritual development of young *Chassidim*.

Matzoh (pl. **matzos**). Unleavened bread. Eaten on Passover in place of leavened bread.

Megillah. Scroll or roll. The Book of Esther is popularly referred to by this name.

Melava malka (pl. **melavei malka**). lit. Escorting the Queen. Applied to the meal and the special festivities after the termination of the Sabbath. Jewish tradition compares the Sabbath to a "Queen".

Menahel (pl. **Menahelim**). Administrator(s).

Mesechta. lit. *Talmudic* tractate. Usually relating to a section of *Gemorrah*.

Mesibos Shabbos. Sabbath meeting.

Mesiras nefesh. Self-sacrifice; complete devotion to an ideal.

Mezuzah (pl. **Mezuzos**). The sacred scroll, containing portions of the *Shema*, affixed on the door-posts of a Jewish home.

Midrash. Rabbinical homiletical literature; exegesis.

Mikvah (pl. **Mikvaos**). lit. A gathering of waters. For ritual immersion.

Mincha. Afternoon prayers.

Minhag. Custom.

Mishna (pl. **Mishnayos**). The codification, by Rabbi Judah Hanassi, of the Oral Law.

Misnagid (pl. **misnagdim**). lit. Opponent(s). Generally used to denote opponents to *chassidus*.

Mittler Rebbe. Rabbi Dovber, son of Rabbi Shneur Zalman, the founder of *Chabad*, was popularly known as the *Mittler Rebbe* (intermediate Rebbe, i.e. the middle one of the first three generations of the fathers of *Chabad*).

Mitzraim. Egypt.

Mitzvah (pl. **mitzvos**). Commandment(s); religious obligation(s), good deed(s).

Mokom. Place.

Moshe Rabbeinu. Moses, our teacher.

Moshiach. Messiah.

Moshol (pl. **mesholim**). Parable(s).

Motzei Tisha B'Av. Immediately following the termination of *Tisha B'Av*.

Mussar. Reproof, ethics, morals. Literature stressing piety and refinement of character.

Nassi. Prince, President. The chief of the Great Sanhedrin in Jerusalem. Used to denote head of Jewry.

Nigleh. Revealed *Torah*, as distinct from *Nistar*.

Nigun (pl. **nigunim**). Melody (melodies).

Nissan. Spring month in the Hebrew calendar.

Nistar. lit. Hidden. Mysticism; esoteric, i.e. *Kabbalah*.

Nosan lonoo Toras Emes vechayai olom nota besoichainoo. Who has given us a Law of Truth and has planted everlasting life in our midst.

Olei Regolim. Refers to those participating in the three Pilgrim Festivals, i.e. *Pesach, Shovuos* and *Succos*. See *Shalosh Regolim.*

Oneg Shabbat (pl. **onegei Shabbat**). Sabbath delight. The *Oneg Shabbat* usually takes place on Friday night or Saturday afternoon. Many organizations and institutions hold *Oneg Shabbat* celebrations which consist of singing, debating, lectures, etc.; refreshments are served.

Ooforatzto. "And you shall spread out." (Gen. 28:14). Lubavitch motto for disseminating *Torah* and *mitzvos* with *Chassidic* enthusiasm.

Parnossa. lit. Sustenance. Livelihood.

Pesach. Passover; begins on the eve of *Nissan* 15.

Pidyon (pl. **pidyonos**). lit. Redemption. Term used for note(s) of request given to a Rebbe. The contents contain the name of the supplicant, the name of his mother and his request.

Pilpul. Method of *Talmudic* study, consisting of examining all arguments of a given text, often involving reconciliation of apparent contradictory texts. The method is usually a means of sharpening the wit and increasing the erudition of the student.

Poskim. Codifiers. Authoritative decisions in the *Halachah*.

Purim. Feast of Lots or Feast of Esther. *Adar* 14.

Raishis Chochmah. lit. Beginning of Wisdom. Book written by Eliyahu ben Moshe Davidosh; lived in Safed and was buried in Hebron *c.* 5332. He was a *talmid* of the *Ramak*. *Raishis Chochmah* teaches *Yiras Hashem*. This volume was studied by the *Alter Rebbe*'s *Chassidim*.

Ramak. (1522–1570). Kabbalist. Name by which Moses ben Jacob Cordovero was known. He was a pupil of Joseph Caro and was chief of the Safed mystics before the advent of Isaac Luria.

Rambam. *RaMBaM*, the popular name by which Rabbi Moshe ben Maimon (Moses Maimonides, 1135–1204) is known. Greatest Jewish philosopher and Codifier of the Middle Ages and distinguished physician. Among his numerous writings his two greatest literary works are his *Code Mishneh Torah* (*Repetition of the Law*) and his philosophical work *Moreh Nevuchim* (*Guide for the Perplexed*). These two works have left an indelible mark on Jewish life and scholarship. As a tribute to his greatness it was said of him that: "From Moses unto Moses there arose none like Moses."

RaShaB. The fifth Lubavitcher Rebbe, Rabbi Sholom Dovber is referred to by Lubavitch *Chassidim* as the *RaShaB*.

RaShBI. Rabbi Shimon ben Yochai, author of the *Zohar*, is popularly known as the *RaShBI*.

Rav. Teacher. Rabbi Shneur Zalman, founder of *Chabad*, was popularly known as the *Rav*.

Rebbe. Rabbi and teacher. Leader of a *Chassidic* group.

Rebbetzin. Wife of a *Rebbe* or Rabbi.

Rishon Le Zion. Title given to the Chief Rabbi of the *Sephardi* community of *Eretz Yisroel*.

Rosh Chodesh. First day of a Hebrew month.

Rosh Hashonoh. Beginning of the Jewish year. First and second days of *Tishrei. Rosh Hashonoh* is the two-day festival at the beginning of the Jewish New Year.

Rosh Yeshivah (pl. **Roshei Yeshivos**). Dean(s) of *yeshivah* (*yeshivos*).

Sabra (pl. **sabras**). Hebrew term applied to the native-born of Israel. It is in fact the name of a cactus plant of Israel. The fruit is prickly on the outside but sweet and good-tasting.

Seder. lit. Order. The Passover banquet is called "*Seder*" because it follows a traditional order of ceremonies, symbols and prayers found in the *Haggadah*.

Sefer (pl. **seforim**). Book(s) of religious content.

Sefer Torah (pl. **Sifrei Torah**). Scroll(s) of the Law.

Sephardi (pl. **Sephardim**). Pertaining to Jews of Spanish or Portuguese origin. Even after the expulsion of Jews from Spain and Portugal at the end of the fifteenth century, the *Sephardi* Jews, in whichever countries they settled, preserved their own ritual, traditions and customs, and their own dialect called Ladino. They use the *Sephardi* pronunciation of Hebrew, which is basically that which is used in Israel.

Shabbos (pl. **Shabbosos**). Sabbath(s), Saturday(s).

Shacharis. The morning prayers.

Shalach monos. The sending of gifts to friends on *Purim*.

Shalom. Peace. Customary Hebrew greeting used in Israel.

Shalom Aleichem. Peace upon you. Well known Hebrew greeting.

Shalosh Regolim. The three Pilgrim Festivals: *Pesach*, *Shovuos* and *Succos*. In Temple times it was customary to go to Jerusalem for these festivals in order to offer sacrifices.

Shamash. The beadle or sexton of a synagogue. The term is used also to denote the additional candle used in kindling the *Chanukah* lights.

Shas. Initial letters of *Shishah Sedorim*, the "Six Orders" of the *Mishna*. The term *Shas* refers to the entire *Talmud*.

Shehecheyanu. "Who has kept us alive" (to this season). Hebrew word contained in the benediction pronounced by Jews on many important occasions, e.g. on tasting fruit for the first time in season; on putting on new clothes; on the first nights of Jewish festivals; before sounding the *Shofar*; before lighting the candle on the first night of *Chanukah*; before reading the *Megillah*.

Sheloh. The initials of the chief book (*Shnei Luchos Ha Bris—Two Tablets of the Covenant*) written by Isaiah Horowitz (*c.* 1556–1630), scholar and *Kabbalist* and the name by which he is popularly known. This was an ethical work, with *Kabbalistic* tendencies, on Jewish laws and customs. It opposed *pilpul* and advocated the study of Hebrew grammar.

Shema. lit. Hear. Passage of the *Chumash* recited daily, in the morning and evening. (Deut. 6:4–9.)

Shemura matzos. Guarded *matzos*; hand-baked *matzos*.

Shevat. The fifth month of the Jewish calendar, corresponding to January/February.

Shiur (pl. **shiurim**). Lesson(s).

Shlito. May he live for many good days.

Shochet (pl. **shochetim**). Ritual slaughterer(s).

Shofar. Ram's horn sounded during the month of *Elul*, on *Rosh Hashonoh* and at the close of *Yom Kippur*.

Shovuos. Feast of Weeks; also known as Pentecost. Observed on the sixth and seventh days of *Sivan*. One of the three Pilgrimage Festivals. Commemorates the giving of the *Torah* on Mount Sinai. This festival also has agricultural significance and the *Book of Ruth*, reminiscent of Jewish agricultural life and of Ruth's acceptance of the Jewish faith, is read on *Shovuos*. *Shovuos* is also the date of the birth and death of King David, the descendant of Ruth.

Shul (Yiddish). Synagogue.

Shulchan Aruch. lit. "Set table". Code of *Torah* Law, compiled by Rabbi Joseph Caro (1488–1575). *Talmud* presents the broad discussion of the law, the background, while the *Shulchan Aruch* is a "set table", an orderly presentation of practical law and usage, regulating every aspect of the Jew's daily life and conduct.

Sichah (pl. **sichos**). A talk; talks.

Siddur (pl. **Siddurim**). Prayer book(s).

Sidra. Weekly portion of the *Torah* read at public services in synagogues. There are fifty-four such portions thereby permitting the reading of the entire *Torah* annually.

Simcha. Joy. Feast or celebration connected with some *mitzvah* or happy family occasion.

Simchas Torah. Festival of Rejoicing with the *Torah*, celebrated on *Tishrei* 23 in the Diaspora and on *Tishrei* 22 in Israel.

Sivan. A month in the Hebrew calendar; third from *Nissan*.

Siyum. Termination; completion. Applied to the completion of the writing of a *Sefer Torah* or more particularly the learning of a tractate of the *Talmud*. Both are recognised occasions for joyful celebration. In the former case a few lines are left in outline which are completed at the *siyum*. In the latter, a special meal is held at which a *hadran* (conclusion lecture) is delivered. First-born often forgo their traditional fast on Passover-eve by organising the celebration of a *Talmudic Siyum* on that day.

Sofer (pl. **sofrim**). Scribe(s).

Succos. Festival of Tabernacles, begins *Tishrei* 15.

Tallis (pl. **taleisim**). Prayer shawl(s) worn by men during morning worship and during *Yom Kippur*.

Talmid (pl. **talmidim**). Pupil(s).

Talmid Chochom (pl. **Talmidei chachomim**). *Talmudic* scholar(s) of high reputation.

Talmud. Post-Biblical Rabbinical literature, including *Mishna* and later teachings, concluded around sixth century of the common era.

Talmud Torah (pl. **Talmud Torahs**). Hebrew school(s) provided by the community, as distinct from the private *cheder*.

Talmudic. Appertaining to the *Talmud*.

Talmudist. One who studies the *Talmud*.

Tammuz. Month of the Hebrew calendar. Falls in the summer.

Tanya. Famous philosophical work, by Rabbi Shneur Zalman of Ladi, in which the principles of *Chabad* are expounded. The name is derived from the initial word of this work. Also called *Likutei Amarim*.

Tefillah. Prayer.

Tefillin. Phylacteries worn by men during weekday morning worship; they contain verses from the Bible including *Shema*.

Tehillim. Psalms.

Tenach. Popular name for the Bible. From the three initial letters of *Torah* (Pentateuch), *Neviim* (Prophets) and *Kesuvim* (Holy Writings).

Teshuvah. lit. Return. Turning away from wrongdoing and returning to the ways of righteousness has always been basic to Judaism. *Teshuvah* is constantly stressed in the Bible and rabbinic literature.

Tisha B'Av. Ninth day of *Av*. Observed by Jews as a day of fasting and mourning to commemorate the destruction of the First Temple by Nebuchadnezzar and the Second Temple by Titus. This date also commemorates the fall of Betar in 135 C.E., the expulsion of the Jews from Spain in 1492 and other national calamities. The *Book of Lamentations* and *Kinos* are recited on *Tisha B'Av*. As an expression of sorrow, worshippers sit without shoes on the floor of the synagogue or on low stools. *Tefillin* are only worn during the afternoon prayers. All ornamentation is temporarily removed from the synagogue.

Tishrei. A month in the Hebrew calendar; following *Elul*.

Tmimim. lit. Whole ones. The name given to *talmidim* of Lubavitch *yeshivos*.

Torah. Used variously for *Chumash*, especially in scroll form, or for the entire body of Jewish religious Law (Bible, *Talmud*, *Midrash*, etc.).

Torah-Or. lit. *Torah* is light.

Toras Chaim. Law of life.

Toras Emes. Law of truth.

Tzaddik (pl. **Tzaddikim**). Righteous man (men).

Tzemach Tzedek. lit. Seed of righteous. Famed *Halachic* and Responsa work by Rabbi Menachem Mendel, third generation of *Chabad* leaders. The author is usually referred to as the "*Tzemach Tzedek*" after the name of his great work. Sages of Israel are often better known by their works than by their personal names.

Uvo Letzion. lit. And there shall come to Zion . . . (a redeemer). Opening words of part of the liturgy recited during daily morning prayers and during the afternoon prayers on Sabbath and Holy Days.

Vehachai yitain el liboh. And the one who is alive should take it to his heart.

Veyidgoo lorov bekerev haaretz. "They should multiply in the Land." (Gen. 48:16.)

V'Torah-Or. And *Torah* is light.

Yahrzeit (Yiddish). "Year time". Anniversary of a death.

Yechidus. Private interview (with the Rebbe).

Yeshivah (pl. **yeshivos**). Advanced school(s) of *Talmudic* Studies. In the U.S.A. it is used in reference to Jewish Day School(s).

Yeshivah gedoloh. Advanced *yeshivah*.

Yeshivah ketanah. *Yeshivah* for younger students.

Yetzias Mitzraim. Liberation from Egypt.

Yiddish. Jewish language.

Yiddishkeit. Jewishness. A term covering the traditional culture of Jewry.

Yiras Hashem. Fear (awe) of G–d.

Yiras Shomayim. Fear (awe) of Heaven.

Yishuv. lit. Settlement. Popularly applied to the Jewish community in the Holy Land.

Yom Kippur. Day of Atonement; *Tishrei* 10.

Yom Tov (pl. **Yomim Tovim**). Feast(s); festival(s).

Yud beis Tammuz. *Tammuz* 12. The festival of *yud beis Tammuz* commemorates the release from prison of the sixth Lubavitcher Rebbe, Rabbi Joseph Isaac Schneersohn. The Rebbe שליט״א *farbrengs* on this date.

Yud Kislev. *Kislev* 10. The festival of *Yud Kislev* commemorates the release from prison of the *Mittler Rebbe*.

Yud Shevat. *Shevat* 10. Anniversary of the death of the sixth Lubavitcher Rebbe, Rabbi Joseph Isaac Schneersohn. The Rebbe שליט״א *farbrengs* on this date.

Yud tes Kislev. *Kislev* 19. The festival of *Yud tes Kislev* commemorates the release from prison of Rabbi Shneur Zalman of Ladi, founder of *Chabad*. The Rebbe שליט״א *farbrengs* on this date and there are celebrations throughout the *Chabad* community.

Zechus. Merit.

Zeman. Term; time.

Zohar. Classic *Kabbalistic* work by Rabbi Shimon ben Yochai.

Acknowledgements

The article "First Chassidic Aliyah" was written by Rabbi Dr. N. Mindel, who acknowledges his indebtedness to Rabbi Chanoch Glitzenstein of Jerusalem for his co-operation in preparing the data. Parts were based on articles by Rabbi Shimon Glitzenstein, Betzalel Landau and Tuvia Blau, which originally appeared in *Bitaon Chabad*.

Especial thanks are due to:

Baruch Nachshon, noted Israeli artist, for his original artwork and valuable collaboration;

Miss Geula Cohen, for permission to publish a translation of parts of her article which appeared in the Israeli evening newspaper *Maariv*;

Rabbi C. Glitzenstein and Rabbi E. Wolff of Israel and Rabbi L. Groner and Rabbi Y. Krinsky of the U.S.A., for making available material for this volume;

Rabbi I. H. Sufrin of London, for his painstaking care in reading the proofs and for his many valuable suggestions;
and

Rabbi N. Sudak, Principal of the Lubavitch Foundation of Great Britain, who was present in Israel at the inception of this volume and who, throughout its compilation, gave valuable and learned assistance and guidance.

NOTE

The traditional way of writing G–d's name (with a dash) has been used throughout this publication. The sources of this tradition are to be found in the *Shulchan Aruch*, *Yoreh Deah*, Chapters 179 and 276 and commentaries. *Rav's Shulchan Aruch*, *Orach Chaim*, Chapter 85, par. 3.

Further Reading

RABBI SHNEUR ZALMAN OF LADI, Vol. I Biography, by Nissan Mindel. 1969.

LIKUTEI AMARIM (TANYA), by Rabbi Shneur Zalman, Part I. Translated with Introduction by Nissan Mindel. 1962.

—PART II—SHAAR HAYICHUD VEHAEMUNAH. Translated with Introduction by Nisen Mangel. 1965.

—PART III—IGERES HATESHUVA. Translated with Introduction by Zalman I. Posner. 1965.

—PART IV—IGERES HAKODESH. Translated with Introduction by Jacob I. Schochet. 1968.

—PART V—KUNTRES ACHRON. Translated by Zalman I. Posner. 1968.

MEMOIRS, by Rabbi Joseph I. Schneersohn. Translated by Nissan Mindel. Volumes I–II. 1956; 1960.

SOME ASPECTS OF CHABAD CHASSIDISM, by Rabbi Joseph I. Schneersohn. Translated with Biographical Sketch by Nissan Mindel. 1961.

ON THE TEACHINGS OF CHASSIDUS, by Rabbi Joseph I. Schneersohn. Translated with Supplements by Zalman I. Posner. 1959.

ON LEARNING CHASSIDUS, by Rabbi Joseph I. Schneersohn. Translated with Supplements by Zalman I. Posner. 1961.

THE "TZEMACH TZEDEK" AND THE HASKALAH MOVEMENT, by Rabbi Joseph I. Schneersohn. Translated with Supplements by Zalman I. Posner. 1962.

THE COMMANDMENTS, by Nissan Mindel. 1961.

RABBI SHNEUR ZALMAN OF LADI, by Gershon Kranzler. 1959.

ARREST AND LIBERATION OF RABBI SHNEUR ZALMAN OF LADI (The History of Yud-Tes Kislev), by A. C. Glitzenstein. Translated by Jacob I. Schochet. 1964.

MY PRAYER. A commentary on the daily prayers, by Nissan Mindel. 1972.

Published by "Kehot" Publication Society

CHALLENGE. An encounter with Lubavitch-Chabad. 1970.

Published by the Lubavitch Foundation of Great Britain